Raising
Girls

Raising
Girls

Why Girls Are Different—
and How to Help Them
Grow Up Happy and Strong

Gisela Preuschoff
Foreword by Steve Biddulph

CELESTIAL ARTS
Berkeley | Toronto

Celestial Arts
an imprint of Ten Speed Press
PO Box 7123
Berkeley CA 94707
www.tenspeed.com

Distributed in Australia by Simon and Schuster Australia, in Canada by Ten Speed Press Canada, in New Zealand by Southern Publishers Group, in South Africa by Real Books, and in the United Kingdom and Europe by Publishers Group UK.

Originally published in German as *Madchen!* by Beustverlag in 2003. The first English language edition was published in Australia and New Zealand by Finch Publishing in 2004, translated by Christina Janka.

Cover and text design by Chloe Rawlins
Cover photograph courtesy of Sean Doyle
Illustrations by Roy Bisson

Photo credits: Sean Doyle, Vanessa Doyle, Christine Durham, Rex Finch, Vicki Finch, Zoe Finch, Micky Foss, Ros Hey, Debbie Jepson, Jo Lamble, Sulee Ling, Sue Morris, Martha Olson, Rob Rathbone, Emily Smith, Christa Tobin, Naomi Warren.

ISBN 13: 987-1-58761-255-8
ISBN 10: 1-58761-255-0

Library of Congress Cataloging-in-Publication Data on file with the publisher.

First Celestial Arts printing, 2006

2 3 4 5 6 — 10 09 08 07 06

Printed in the United States of America

Contents

Foreword

I remember the moment. It's not an easy memory: I am present at the caesarean delivery of our second child, terrified for my wife's safety, for my own powerlessness to help, and for this little life that is being prised out from the area that lies below the green surgical sheets. And then someone is saying, 'It's a girl!'

And amid the tears of relief are tears of joy, too, that catch me utterly by surprise. Our son is already seven years old; this new baby is long awaited. But had anyone asked me hours before, I would have given the old clichéd answer, 'I don't care what sex it is, as long as it's healthy.'

So why am I so happy? What had I been hiding from myself? A girl is something else—special to me as a man, wonderful in a different way to how a son is wonderful—and I will spend the rest of my life grappling with this, and happy to grapple, knowing it's one of life's gifts, a child who will become and then be a woman, and always, whatever happens, my daughter.

For a father, a daughter is something powerful. For a mother, equally so, but for quite different reasons, and we rarely feel this so intensely as in the moment they are born. And so we sit in this place halfway between feeling so lucky, so blessed, and so terrified about getting it wrong and not being up to the job.

For help, we tap into one of the things that our culture does well—books, ideas, discussion—to help us broaden our picture and learn from the lives of others. We don't have elders, we don't have a village to help us. But at least we have a questioning society that brings us theories and ideas from across the globe, all for us to digest, use or discard.

This book gets beneath the surface of you and me as parents of girls, because much of the trouble we still have with girls has its roots deep in our own experience, the wounded experience of growing up in a terrible century. Many of us, men and women, had difficult times growing up. Distant fathers did not teach us how to father, while marital chaos and widespread divorce made us distrustful and unsure of how to form strong relationships and make them work. Few of us had deep or meaningful spiritual influence or guidance. Many traditional religions had either shrunk dramatically or been replaced by the seductive and pervasive pleasures that money could buy. We didn't really know the deep peace of the earth and sky around us, only the chatter of television and the clutter of rooms full of stuff.

What we want to give our daughters, we often don't even have ourselves. But the search is on. A baby girl in our arms, soft skin, bright eyes, sharp intelligence wanting to grow and reach out, calls to us strongly to get our act together, to focus and go looking for the tools and understanding we will need.

This book is written by a woman on her own search and contains much that will stir up your thinking. Rather than giving you formulae, lists, bullet points and glib advice (the sure sign of a third-rate parenting 'expert'), Gisela inspires you to search deeply within. Things you may have kept buried inside will come to the surface—beliefs, passions, forgotten memories—that can help you to be a more wide awake, fully alive human being rather than a someone who merely provides meals, drives carpool, and packs book bags for another school day. What our kids will remember, and what will strengthen them, is the moments of closeness, honesty, and peace that we spend amid the scramble of life, the parts that we fence off and make special, where we refuse to dance to the commercial world's tune, and tend a garden for love to grow.

Things have gotten better for girls. We need to remember this. Cultural pressures in the first half of the twentieth century crippled girls with narrow social and career role possibilities, just as it pressured boys to be the brave soldier, the aloof father, the home tyrant, the frustrated wage slave.

We had a revolution in the 1960s and 70s, and now girls can do anything they want to, though it's turning out to be not quite so simple. The empire struck back, and the ugly forces of commercial greed rushed into the vacuum created by the collapse of old values, and created for girls other forms of slavery. Today, you have to be slender, but you also have to have big breasts (even if it means cutting open your chest and implanting slabs of silicone). You have to choose a career, even if you simply yearn for some peace and quiet with your new baby, or to be creative, or have some time to just be. You have to *want* to have it all.

We've made progress, but as this excellent book points out, we have a long way still to go. For instance, there is a lot being learned about girls:

✦ The first year or so of life is one of such rapid brain growth that everything important seems to be moving into place inside that little head and heart—the ability to love, to feel safe and relaxed, the ability to connect with another human being in empathy and trust—all happen during the first year.

✦ The world we live in can be very toxic to young children, from the food on supermarket shelves to the messages delivered by an insensitive and manipulative media. As parents we must monitor what we put into her body *and* her mind.

✦ We parents have cultural baggage and psychological wounds of our own that we may unwittingly pass on to our daughters. I don't want to scare you, but simply remind you that children readily pick up on our emotional state, whether we intend it or not.

✦ The conventional twentieth-century idea of the father as the distant breadwinner has done enormous harm. We now know that fathers play an irreplaceable part in the confidence and self-esteem building of girls, a delicate role involving affection without invasion, fun combined with firmness, and care with empowering levels of trust and freedom. Current research on everything from anorexia to career choice, from sexual safety to educational opportunity, shows that a loving, involved dad makes a world of difference to his daughter.

✦ By mistaking equality for sameness, we have caused much harm. Boys and girls grow differently, and should not be lumped together and expected to thrive. In secondary schools, especially, there are

important reasons for separating girls from boys
into classrooms where both sexes can be free from
vulnerability to and pressure from the opposite sex;
and free to learn and explore their fragile new iden-
tities without falling into the stereotypical and
defensive pretence of being macho or sexy, cute
or coy, aggressive or smart.

Your daughter may be a newborn, a toddler, or already in
school. She may be a teenager, vulnerable but with a growing
identity and sense of selfhood. She may be a young woman,
relating to men, making her own way in the world, needing you
less and less, or so it may seem. She may even be a mother herself, coming to you with a new awareness of what you share. The
more open you are to the wonderful daughter in your life, the
more you will have to give her. Your parenthood never ends.

—Steve Biddulph

Introduction

I would like to stimulate you to reflect with this book. What is really special about having a girl as a child? What kind of woman should your daughter grow into? How important this consideration really is can be illustrated by the following results from a classic research study in which a group of male and female babies were randomly dressed in pink or light blue jumpsuits. When a group of dads was asked to observe and describe the children, the 'pink' babies were invariably described as 'fragile, pretty, sweet and cute,' although there were boys among them; in contrast, the 'light blue' infants (girls included) were described as 'healthy, sturdy, strong and attentive.'

People react differently to a male baby than to a female baby. And that's quite normal, for there are, of course, differences. These assumptions are not only biologically conditioned but are based on social influences, expectations and premises. In fact, there has always been something like a 'girl culture' or a culture of the feminine in all cultures around the world and at all times throughout history. We can resist it, but never quite withdraw from it.

Only when, as parents, we become aware of which images and ideas of femininity we carry inside us, and which of these images are socially effective, can we take a critical look at them, perhaps argue about them and even take a new one, or turn back onto the well-established paths.

What do you want for your daughter? From what age is she to become 'a girl'? How many months or years old will she be before she wears her first jewelry? And when should her ears be pierced? Some parents have very definite ideas about this, and no one will be able to dissuade them. Others have not thought about it at all, but probably carry unconscious notions around with them.

However, one thing should remain clear from the start: children are not putty in our hands. They belong to themselves and bring their own unique personalities into the world. As their parents, we are lucky to be allowed to accompany them for a while. In order for this journey to be successful, it's also important that we understand our roles as mother and father.

Each child is, in my eyes, a wonderful and unique gift. But individual differences notwithstanding, there are recognizable differences between the sexes. Women, for example, have more acute hearing than men and can better distinguish high tones, which also happen to be the frequencies that babies use when they cry. After just a week, a female infant can distinguish her mother's voice, as well as the crying of another baby located in the same room, from other noises. Boys cannot do this. Moreover, females perceive visual detail better, a skill that is of great significance in a toddler's environment.

These days, new research is revealing important differences between girls and boys, men and women. Are they biologically inherited or socially conditioned?

I believe that parents of a girl should pay special attention to their own internal images, expectations and prejudices. They should ask themselves, 'What does it mean to me that I have a daughter?'

This is very important, as it can help parents avoid burdening the child with a hidden agenda, for example, by saying, 'She should on no account become like my mother' or 'She's not allowed to become as spoiled as my sister' or 'She'll have to learn to assert herself'. Parents can then choose *consciously* either to stick with or distance themselves from these notions. This, in turn, gives their daughter the opportunity either to reject or embrace such parental expectations.

Whether you have a son or a daughter, apart from wishing for a child who is born healthy, it does seem to make a difference. The decisive questions we should ask ourselves are, 'What do we conclude from the gender of our child, and how do we deal with this?'

Even today, the issue of 'boy or girl' still plays a significant role in family planning all over the world. For example, according to surveys in Europe, more couples wish for a girl, not a boy, as their first child, possibly in the hope that a daughter would be more likely to look after her aging parents in later years. While in China, where parents are permitted to have one child, there is an ancient cultural preference to have a boy. This accounts for the widespread termination of female fetuses, and for the large numbers of female children being adopted by non-Chinese families.

Were you planning for a girl? If so, why? If not, how did you feel when a baby daughter suddenly entered your life? These are important questions that influence how you view your task of raising a girl. Compare your answers with those of your partner, as well as your own parents, your partner's parents and some close friends. The aggregate of opinions relates to a very important issue: projection. By this I don't mean slide shows in the living room, but rather how we often project our own beliefs, attitudes, biases and expectations on to others, often mistakenly and often unconsciously. If you can become more aware of your ideas regarding these matters, you will be less likely to project your thoughts on to others, including your daughter.

Try the following exercise to really get you thinking!

Self-awareness for parents

Here are some questions for you to consider. They are about you as a child, you as a parent, and a few are about your daughter. Toss them around in your mind, or write down your answers for future reference (which I would recommend). If you choose to write them down, keep the answers someplace private. Both you and your daughter's other parent should complete this exercise. Just ignore the gender words that don't apply to you. When you have answered all the questions and developed a relatively clear profile of yourself and your own childhood, talk about these things with your daughter. This conversation is likely to stay with you for many years to come.

Then

✦ When you were a girl/boy, what did you look like?

✦ What were your favorite clothes?

✦ What toys did you have? What games did you play?

✦ What was your personality as a child? Were you shy or outgoing?

✦ What did you like about being a girl/boy?

✦ What did you find difficult about being a girl/boy?

✦ What were you not allowed to do as a girl/boy?

✦ What duties and chores did you have?

✦ Who were your role models?

✦ What was your greatest dream?

✦ What kinds of things did you often imagine?

✦ Can you remember any special praise or compliments you received as a child?

✦ Can you remember insulting comments directed at you as a child?

✦ On which occasions were you especially excited or thrilled?

✦ On which occasions were you especially sad or frightened?

Now

✦ In which situations do you behave like a 'typical' female/male?

- ✦ Which qualities do you particularly like in girls?

- ✦ Which qualities do you particularly like in boys?

- ✦ Which qualities do you particularly admire in your daughter?

- ✦ What do you wish for your daughter?

- ✦ Which aspects of her life are you most happy about?

I hope that this book provides you with concrete guidelines on how to approach your daughter's upbringing. I have drawn on experiences with my own daughter, scientific findings, as well as the experiences of other parents derived from my own research and consulting work. I have thought of the little girl I once was, and all the girls and women I have known during my life.

Fathers and brothers also play a crucial role in raising girls. The experiences a girl has with the male members of her family will follow her all her life. Just as there is no loud without soft, no light without dark, and no large without small—there are no daughters without fathers, even when the latter, for whatever reason, live separately from their daughter and/or have completely broken off contact.

You have a girl and she is a gift (in the truest sense of that word). It really matters how this gift is nourished and nurtured, and I would like to accompany you on this wonderful journey from infancy to womanhood. My hope is to point out pitfalls and challenges and *prevent* them. But above all, I would like to reveal a joyful pathway to cooperation between parent and parent, and parent and child. In addition, I would like this book to be a journey of self-discovery during which you may recognize what glorious opportunities the birth of a girl offers you personally.

Chapter 1

Why Girls Are Different

All parents worry about their children. We want to do our very best for them—or at least avoid the really big mistakes. These days, our expectations of our sons will be very similar to the expectations we have of our daughters. We want our children to be strong—strong in the sense of being socially responsible, independent, somewhat assertive, clever and affectionate. And we want our children to be able to handle all the tasks that they will confront in life.

We're all individuals

Long before a baby sees the light of day, a film is playing in the minds of the parents-to-be; they imagine what their life with the baby will be like, and they often have fixed ideas about the qualities a son and a daughter will have. This is completely normal—it's also fun, and it increases their joy in their child.

While pregnant with her daughter, one woman wrote in her diary, 'I have the feeling that I could just pull the finished picture, which is a perfectly formed little figure inside me, out of a drawer. She has already been born, because my imagination has already shaped her; she's a beautiful, strong, self-confident, lively and intelligent creature.' On the other hand, the father of this little girl imagined a lovely, sweet, affectionate little girl he could snuggle with and cuddle.

Parents should try to remember that there are many prejudices with regard to the sexes, and that most children develop quite differently from what their parents imagined in their dreams. Girls are by no means always calm, loving and well-behaved, just as boys are not automatically naughty, aggressive and tough. Each child is unique. Each child brings a distinctive personality into the world, and each is shaped by her or his environment.

Most women who know they are expecting a baby girl identify completely with the unborn child. They see the baby as a miniature version of themselves and feel a strong symbiosis with the child in their belly: 'We're the same—we want the same things and are interested in the same things.'

The biological story

What do the biological facts say? In the first weeks of pregnancy, when women as a rule don't even know they are pregnant, male and female embryos are identical. They are only distinguishable through their sex chromosomes: XY for boys and XX for girls. The X chromosome originates from the egg cell of the mother, and the father's sperm has either an X or a Y. If the egg is fertilized by an X sperm, it will be a girl; if not, it will be a boy. Most genes lie in the X chromosomes, of which there are around 2,000, among them the so-called 'intelligence gene.' The reproductive genes romp around within the Y chromosomes.

Statistically, more boys than girls are conceived, however more male than female fetuses are miscarried, or stillborn. No one knows exactly why this is so. One theory suggests that male fetuses may be more sensitive to harmful environmental factors, another that the mother's immune system classifies the male fetus as 'foreign' and attacks it in error.

During the sixth week of pregnancy, the male Y chromosome gives the command to form male gonads; the X chromosome of the developing baby girl only induces ovary development from the twelfth week. During the course of the pregnancy, ovaries and gonads excrete sex hormones, which are involved in the formation of physical characteristics and also influence future behavior.

The 'male' sex hormones are called androgens, and include testosterone; the 'female' hormones are estrogen and progesterone. These hormones occur in both the male and female organisms, although in differing quantities. When psychologists talk about a woman's 'inner male' and about a man's 'feminine side', that is exactly what they mean. We all have male and female parts within us, and it is sensible to use both!

If the embryo has enough androgens, a penis grows and the female sex organs waste away

and disappear. A vagina, fallopian tubes and womb will grow in the female embryo, and the male sex organs will die off. The fallopian tubes of the female embryo already store 6–7 million eggs, but by the onset of puberty this number will fall to 400,000. On the other hand, boys only produce sperm during puberty.

What's between their ears?

With sexual differentiation, male and female embryo brains start to develop differently. The clearest distinction can be seen in the hypothalamus, the hormonal center or 'relay station' of the front and middle brain. From here, numerous bodily functions, including sexual arousal, hunger, thirst, feeling hot or cold, and fight-or-flight reactions are regulated. Here there is also a pinhead-sized cluster of cells, the so-called 'third interstitial nucleus of the anterior hypothalamus'. It is thought that this area controls sexual desire. The size of this cell cluster is identical for boys and girls when they are infants, but it begins to grow in boys from the age of ten; and by the onset of puberty, boys have two and a half times more nerve cells in this region than girls.

The most often debated difference between the male and female brain, however, concerns the band of nerve cells connecting the right and left cerebral hemispheres. This bridge, called the corpus callosum, is definitely larger in the female brain, and it may explain differences between male and female thought processes. Girls and women use both cerebral hemispheres simultaneously, while males use only one at a time.

It has also been proven that a girl's left cerebral hemisphere matures more quickly than a boy's. Because the speech center resides in this hemisphere, boys, as a rule, learn to speak later than girls. The right cerebral hemisphere, which is responsible

for the solution of spatial-visual problems, develops later in girls, which is why young girls often have difficulty imagining objects from different perspectives and orienting themselves spatially.

✦ ✦ ✦ ✦ ✦ ✦ ✦ ✦ ✦ ✦ ✦ ✦ ✦ ✦ ✦ ✦ ✦ ✦ ✦ ✦

Birth differences

As a rule, the birth of a boy lasts on average an hour and a half longer than that of a girl, possibly because boys have an average 5 percent greater body weight at birth than girls. If a girl seems very contented as an infant, for example, it may be because her birth went smoothly without traumatic experiences. In 1987 in Finland, it was established that newborn boys had a 20 percent greater risk of low Apgar scores than girls. (The Apgar system is an index developed by the American doctor Virginia Apgar, which measures a newborn's vital signs, including respirations, pulse, color, appearance, and reflexes.) Premature births, vulnerability to mental disturbances and infections, and likelihood of accidents are all distinctly lower with girls than with boys. We can only speculate about all the factors that contribute to this imbalance, but we can say that cortisol, the 'stress' hormone, and testosterone, which builds up in boys, heighten the vulnerability of the immune system in male infants.

Perhaps the fact that girls are more socially attuned after birth and maintain eye contact longer than boys is connected to this higher probability of good health for them. They also react more strongly to noises and to the presence of other people, cry less often and are pacified more easily.

✦ ✦ ✦ ✦ ✦ ✦ ✦ ✦ ✦ ✦ ✦ ✦ ✦ ✦ ✦ ✦ ✦ ✦ ✦

Even during pregnancy, the female body is three weeks ahead of the male in terms of bone development. At birth, female babies are already four to six weeks ahead of boys developmentally. And by puberty, most girls are visibly at least two years ahead of their male classmates.

Developmental differences and consequences

Female skin is significantly thinner than male skin and seems to want touching more. The hormone that releases the need to be touched is oxytocin. It is no wonder that women, whose receptors are ten times more sensitive than men's, feel it is so important to touch and hug their husbands, children and friends.

Parents tend to speak more often to their female babies, which certainly could explain why girls seem to listen more attentively. As little girls maintain eye contact longer than boys, they 'demand' that their parents devote more time and attention to them, smile at them and talk to them.

Every baby begins to distinguish female voices from male voices very early on. She knows her parents' voices from the time she was in the womb. With this, a more detailed classification process begins: for example, a deep voice means coarser facial features and rougher skin. The baby is gathering information that, years later, molds her image of 'masculine' and 'feminine'.

At the age of six months, little girls are already more independent than their male companions: they can occupy themselves happily with toys and can comfort themselves with a thumb or special blanket.

The most significant difference in the first months is the speed with which little girls mature. Their height and weight increase more quickly, and they cut their canine teeth earlier than boys.

By the age of seven months, most little girls can roll from one side onto the other, they can crawl already, they are skilled at handling a spoon, they can draw lines and they can pull up a zipper.

These developmental differences continue apace. By pre-school age, a girl's fine motor skills are significantly better developed. Girls also start speaking much sooner and have more self-control (see page 37).

Parental expectations and behavior

So we see there are distinct, biologically determined differences between boys and girls. These are encouraged or diluted by their parents' behavior and the comprehensive environment around them. It is intriguing to know that in experiments, adults faced with a group of infants clothed in yellow jumpsuits could not tell whether the babies were boys or girls, even though they claimed they could! As soon as they learned the actual genders of the children, however, they reacted and interacted with the girls differently from the boys.

In the 1980s, a young mother recorded in her diary a remark made by one of her girlfriends on seeing her newborn baby daughter, 'Katie will be able to twist men around her little finger.' And the mother herself was sure that 'To exist in this world of men, a woman must look good.'

Is this still true these days? Absolutely. The pressure to be fashionably beautiful has never been as great as it is today, and girls suffer more than boys if they don't conform. I shall return to this later in the book.

Almost everyone notices that parents dress and groom their little daughters particularly carefully. A little girl's 'natural' predisposition to primp and tidy herself up is welcomed and reinforced by adults. Female researchers have observed that parents tend to look after their small daughters more tenderly than their small sons. This may have to do with the widespread illusion that boys must be toughened up in order to become successful men, or that they are not as sensitive as girls in the first place. Although males are less *physically* sensitive than females, how did this biological fact become extended to include *emotional* sensitivity?

✦ ✦ ✦ ✦ ✦ ✦ ✦ ✦ ✦ ✦ ✦ ✦ ✦ ✦ ✦ ✦ ✦ ✦ ✦

It's a girl!

There is no doubt that expecting parents spend a lot of time contemplating the sex of their unborn child. It was 1987. My husband and I already had three sons, and I was pregnant again. 'If it's going to be a boy again, I'd like to prepare myself for it,' I thought, 'and if it's a girl, I shall be especially glad—I can't deny it.'

For this reason I had an amniocentesis test (which nowadays has been widely replaced by an ultrasound scan), although I gave a great deal of thought to its side effects and implications. Would I wish to abort the child if it wasn't healthy? Luckily, I didn't have to answer this question. I did, however, become conscious of the fact that, deep inside, I had decided in favor of the child regardless of the outcome of the test.

I gave birth to a healthy girl! Significantly, though, I was told the gender of the baby when termination of the pregnancy was no longer possible. 'So that children are not terminated because they are the "wrong" sex,' I was advised.

✦ ✦ ✦ ✦ ✦ ✦ ✦ ✦ ✦ ✦ ✦ ✦ ✦ ✦ ✦ ✦ ✦ ✦ ✦

Who *you* are is crucial

Sometimes we forget that who we are affects who our children will become. Thus, self-awareness is crucial for parents. What kind of person am I? How do I behave? What kind of example am I setting for my child? (To help you answer these questions, see page 25.) The better you know yourself and understand your own anxieties, feelings and desires, the less likely you are to force your children into a rigid mold or transfer your biases and anxieties onto them. This means that the most difficult aspect about raising children—whether you have boys or girls or both—is the work you have to do on *yourself.*

When you have a daughter, you must ask yourself what it means to you personally to be part of a female child's upbringing, and what femininity means to you. You need to be honest here. Little children see through insincerity quickly. What does the subject of girls mean to you? Barbie dolls, ruffles and curls, horses, high heels, pink dresses? Or wise women, witches, grandmothers, female presidents, astronauts and taxi drivers? Femininity has many facets today. What is your understanding of it?

Your ideas of femininity

The examples of femininity that are being shown to girls today range from world-famous athletes, politicians, film and television stars, supermodels and celebrities who are famous for being famous to anonymous working moms, stay-at-home moms, single moms and working women who opted to not have children. What matters to you personally? Are you aware of which standards of femininity you respect? Which standards you actually live by? And what tolerance you have for other forms of femininity? If you can truthfully and clearly answer these questions you'll be able to more easily answer all the questions that arise as you bring up your daughter.

Try this exercise: Sit down with your daughter's father (or mother, if you are the father) and make a list (each of you should make your own) of the qualities and skills you value positively in women. If this scenario won't work for you, try to do it with

a friend whose judgment and opinions you trust. Be sure to list as many of your images, expectations, values and prejudices you can think of. For example, do you assume girls 'should' be good at certain school subjects like art and literature? Or 'should' they overcome the popular stereotypes and excel in science and mathematics? Is it better for a girl to be assertive or affectionate? Confident or modest? What does a 'good girl' do? How does a 'bad girl' behave? Should parents make such a distinction at all? Are leadership skills positive female qualities? How about athletic prowess or manual dexterity? Will you feel disappointed if she isn't musical (like you or your spouse)? How do you rate intuition, empathy and the capacity for love? When you've finished, compare your lists.

While you won't be able to force your daughter to embody all the qualities you have written down, it is important that *you* acknowledge and understand your feelings about girls and women. Your daughter will choose her own way, but your attitudes and ideas will also shape her in important ways.

Personality types

For better or worse, girls have been categorized into two principal social types: One type is strong, self-confident, optimistic, able
to deal with and adapt to change and eager to perform; the other
type feels herself at a disadvantage with boys, has a low level of
self-esteem, and sees her future prospects as narrow. Of course,
there are girls who refuse to be slotted into one group or the other
and who follow their own path on the way to their own identity.

Although the last millennium was mainly shaped by men,
more and more women will increasingly play a primary role in
our future. Women already participate in global affairs, but in
what ways might the state of world affairs finally come into balance between the masculine and feminine? Can you imagine
your daughter one day becoming President or winning a Nobel
Prize? Regardless of the path your daughter takes, she already
belongs to a generation of women who will work *with* men to
determine the future of this world.

She will help weave the fabric of human history. So what kind
of a future do you dream of and wish for your daughter? Will you
tell her stories about it? In your opinion, how should women and
men relate to each other in the future? Have you spoken to your
daughter's other parent about this?

What makes girls the way they are?

Female behavior is not only inherited, it is also learned, as every
girl is born into a society where the relations between the sexes are
already firmly established. Moreover, each family has its own culture and it's own history.

For women, our female antecedents are of special significance.
But it's not only girls who need to understand their roots—all

children need this! What do you know about your family? What part of the world did they come from? When did they put down roots in the community? What are their racial and ethnic origins? Are there religious traditions or cultural beliefs that you have adopted or discarded? For instance, do you come from a family with a strong work ethic, or for whom volunteering is a priority? Are there genetic issues to consider? For example, maybe you come from a family haunted by congenital disease. Did you enjoy a secure childhood provided by involved and nurturing parents? Or was it lonesome and stressful due to absence from illness? These are just a few examples of family behavior patterns.

My own view

When I think about what I wish for women who are growing up in the twenty-first century, I think of qualities that have to do with what I call 'original femininity,' values that have largely been lost. I wish for empathy, cooperation, patience, a sense of community, creativity, and for the power of imagination, intuition and wisdom.

The editor of a well-known parenting magazine recently told me that she longed to be a stay-at-home, full-time mother. But she dared not say this aloud at her office or even among her friends. Admitting she loved being at home and looking after her children would brand her a 'reactionary.' But must women have a career outside the home? Do we have to imitate men in order to be taken as seriously and valued as much as men?

For me, femininity is connected to life-giving forces. I don't mean that I believe all women must bear children. Each of us must decide that for herself. But I believe it is important that we devote ourselves to the cause of life: that we speak out against war

and speak up for justice; that we resist violence nonviolently; that we work to preserve nature and resist the destruction of our environment. I believe we must teach our daughters to respect life in all its forms. And I believe we must acknowledge our achievements as women.

Femininity, for me, means giving life, protecting it, going with it—and seeing it pass. It is about recognizing that we are subject to a rhythm, that death is a part of life, that time after time there must be a farewell followed by a new start. Let us show our daughters the moon, for if we observe it closely, we'll know a little of what it's like to live on Earth.

These are my personal beliefs and opinions. But truth is subjective. Do whatever is true to your nature and your convictions—but do it consciously, and in the knowledge that you are a role model for your daughter. If you want her to be a strong woman, she will need strong role models. Being strong means being in harmony with yourself, expressing yourself genuinely, asserting yourself honestly. Being strong means bidding farewell to the victim's role and taking responsibility for yourself, for your beliefs, for your choices. Whoever does not seize her own strength is helpless. You claim your identity through your actions.

Which possibilities do you wish to give your daughter?

The first role models for a girl are her mother and father. If you are mindful, alert, communicative and present, you can't do anything wrong.

In a nutshell

✦ Before we think about how to raise our daughters, we have to know what we ourselves think about girls, women and femininity. Sometimes, we may need to question that, and work to change our thought and behavior patterns.

✦ Remember, other people will have their own reactions and opinions to the news that you are soon to be, or already are, the parents of a baby girl. Be ready for 'advice' you may not be comfortable with!

✦ Newborn girls are different from newborn boys physically, and some of these differences are more pronounced in the first few months of life: girls are likely to want to be touched more than boys; many can play independently and comfort themselves earlier than boys can; they often crawl earlier than boys do.

Boy? Girl? Human! —Leo

When my wife was pregnant for the first time, we decided we didn't want to know the sex of our child before the birth. We wanted the full-on, first-time experience of pregnancy—no tricks of technology, no advance warnings of whether our lives were about to turn a distinct shade of blue or pink. As the weeks passed, we had lots of fun speculating on the boy/girl question: how I would have a willing and long-term football-kicking partner if it were a boy, and how I would protect her innocence against all would-be suitors if it were a girl. The funniest part of all this is that when the wee one actually popped out of my wife's body, both my wife and I were in a state of such transcendental awe that it took us a full minute (okay, maybe a little bit less) to get around to checking what the baby's sex was. In those irreplaceable first few moments of life, we didn't care about anything other than that our baby was there, out, with us at last. She was a girl.

When my wife got pregnant again, we chose to have an ultrasound scan and decided to find out what the fetus's sex was. We wanted to do it differently this time. It was another girl. We stopped at two children, not wanting to push the envelope too far! In hindsight, that process of guessing during the first pregnancy was very special: it was the only time in my life that I might have been about to have a son. Now I have two daughters, and of course I can't imagine it being any other way. But the dreaming was good.

Chapter 2

Developing Your Relationship with Your New Daughter

As soon as your daughter is born, you have a special task to perform: you must say goodbye to your 'dream child' and greet, acknowledge and accept your real one. This may be particularly hard if the infant you are holding in your arms is quite different from the one you expected.

The first step

Step one is to forget your pre-birth expectations. Easy-going charmers who seem calm and serene and look adorable from day one have an easy time of it, even if they don't precisely match their parents' dream version of the perfect baby. A screamer, however, who comes into the world bald and wrinkled and bright red, and who gives the impression of chronic fussiness, presents a few challenges. All your fantasies come

crashing down. Perhaps your newborn is a girl when she 'should' have been a boy. Perhaps she was born too early and carries the risks that come with a premature birth. Perhaps her Apgar scores are disappointingly low or she arrived with obvious disabilities or serious health problems. We certainly don't control everything.

Having said all that, it is also the case that many parents experience exactly the opposite and are overwhelmed by their own capacity to love. They had never expected that a little creature, their beautiful perfect daughter, could inspire so much emotion. They are surprised by the primal, deep force that rolls over them like a huge wave whenever they look at their precious baby.

Bonding: the prerequisite for healthy development

This farewell to the dream child is the first task for brand new parents. Then you can discover what a treasure you have in your real child. Your little girl is the way she is, and she will grow all the better the more you love her. For the first few months of her life, this means being there for her all the time. She needs skin-to-skin, physical contact with you. She needs for you to caress her lovingly and massage her, to nurse her, talk to her, carry her around with you and sleep near her. 'Love' is an action word, and

in the first months with a baby, love is in fact a very strenuous activity. However, it is exactly this loving (and tiring!) behavior that is the foundation for a secure bond between you and your baby. And having a secure bond with her parents in the first few years of her life is a critical requirement for every mental and emotional stage of development she will move through.

✦ ✦ ✦ ✦ ✦ ✦ ✦ ✦ ✦ ✦ ✦ ✦ ✦ ✦ ✦ ✦ ✦ ✦ ✦

The impact of 'attachment theory'

In the 1950s, John Bowlby observed a number of children and orphans whose lives had been traumatically impacted by World War II. His groundbreaking 'attachment theory' is based on this research. This theory states that children can only develop their skills optimally if they have a trusting, secure bond with at least one adult role model. Bowlby's very moving film about a 12-year-old girl who lived all alone in a hospital caused a worldwide sensation. In fact, we have him to thank for several things we take for granted today:

✦ Mothers and newborns are now rarely separated in maternity wards (as they once were routinely) unless the medical condition of the mother or child requires it.

✦ Parents may usually stay with their sick or injured children in hospitals.

✦ Parents are now better informed of how important a stable, close relationship with their child is for her or his future development.

✦ ✦ ✦ ✦ ✦ ✦ ✦ ✦ ✦ ✦ ✦ ✦ ✦ ✦ ✦ ✦ ✦ ✦ ✦ ✦

Premature babies, who must be isolated in the early hours and days of life until their immune systems develop, will grow and thrive with fewer problems if they routinely receive human touch from their parents and medical staff. It is interesting and wonderful to observe a newborn using her purely instinctive communicative skills that enable her to make contact and then form a bond with her mother or father or caretaker. Most parents react intuitively to these signals, and in this way the ties of love are reinforced even more.

If you accept your new daughter as she is, and if you look after her responsibly and give her total security by nestling her little body next to yours, you will be giving her the secure base she needs to flourish. You cannot spoil a baby. She is innocent and defenseless and utterly dependent on your care. If you give her everything she needs, you are doing the absolute best thing for her. Our knowledge about the special powers that babies have, right from birth, has grown dramatically in recent years. But new parents don't need to study any of this; all you need to do is observe your daughter and give her what she wants. Just as the little girl in front of you feels an innate urge to grow and acquire skills and knowledge, you also have the inborn skills to look after your child. Follow your intuition and trust your judgment, and you will do the job properly.

The 'positive mother/father complex'

Psychologist Verena Kast calls this first, close bond with the mother the 'positive mother complex'. There is also a corresponding 'positive father complex'. According to Swiss psychologist Carl Jung, a 'complex' arises from a meaningful interaction between two people. You probably know about the 'inferiority complex' that can develop when a person is systematically devalued by their environment. No person is worth 'less' than another, but when someone is told that they are a failure again and again, they eventually start to believe it. The opposite is also true.

The importance of mothers

Girls who are shaped by a positive mother complex take their right to exist for granted, they are usually creative and can 'live and let live'. They know about everyone's right to receive respect, to express physical and spiritual needs, to seek self-fulfillment and to expect a fair share of worldly goods. They feel uplifted by life, and enjoy their bodies, food, sexuality and the fact of being alive.

Girls eventually need to loosen their close bond to their mother so they can develop their own identity and their own personality can unfold. This task faces them in puberty, unless the mother dies or leaves her family before her daughter reaches adolescence.

The importance of fathers

This inevitable separation from the mother often happens earlier with boys than girls. It's important for a girl to also have her father present in her life from the very beginning so she will develop a healthy, positive father complex. If a girl's early experience includes her father—or a caring male role model—she

will find it easier to detach herself from the mother-child symbiosis. She will also learn that relationships have various shadings: that Mom and Dad treat her differently, and that each parent has a distinctly different personality, diverse opinions, and outlook on the world.

✦ ✦ ✦ ✦ ✦ ✦ ✦ ✦ ✦ ✦ ✦ ✦ ✦ ✦ ✦ ✦ ✦ ✦

What special things do fathers do?

Fathers respond to their children, just like mothers do. But fathers differ in that they often prefer physically stimulating and noisier forms of play, with more physical movement and abrupt changes between active and passive phases of interaction. The play style of fathers is often more exciting than that of mothers, and is highly prized by children.

✦ ✦ ✦ ✦ ✦ ✦ ✦ ✦ ✦ ✦ ✦ ✦ ✦ ✦ ✦ ✦ ✦ ✦

Little girls who have both parents in their lives from the start soon learn different relationship patterns, and to attach different expectations to different relationships. This makes it easier for them to adapt to or get involved in new situations because they already have a broader range of reactions than they would if they were dependent on only one parent. While a little girl experiences her mother as the same as herself, her father radiates the fascination of the stranger (which is significant from the beginning!). Statistics tell us that many very successful women have had fathers who brought them up to be independent and self-sufficient. These women remember their dads as intelligent, ambitious, energetic and tolerant.

Don't give her everything she wants

Many adult women have told me that it's difficult for them to say no, especially to their kids. It's important to be able to say both yes and no to all members of your family. If you accept other people, including your children, as individuals, you also accept that each of you can make personal choices and decisions about all sorts of things.

If your daughter wants cocoa for breakfast and you have none, you'll have to tell her no. She'll be disappointed and she may whine or fuss or cry and demand the cocoa. How do you feel about this? Do you say to yourself, it's normal to be disappointed and to express disappointment verbally? Or do you feel guilty about your

daughter not having everything she wants? Do you get impatient and aggressive with her?

Check your responses in these situations and remind yourself that it's all right to refuse your child something. However, many children live with long lists of rules that, while well-intentioned and designed to keep them from harm, can actually impede their development. Do you encourage or discourage your young daughter from the following?

* climbing trees

* jumping in puddles

* playing in sand or mud

* handling scissors, glue, tape and other tools

* building a fort with boxes

* standing at the stove and cooking something for herself

When sensibly supervised, these are activities that promote neurological development, refine motor skills and give your child a sense of competence and autonomy. On the other hand, if children have no barriers, they lose their orientation. When *everything* is allowed, children become deeply uncertain. Setting limits by saying no to your daughter when she asks to watch television or wear a certain T-shirt doesn't hurt.

You might say no to playing with her if you're exhausted and need a break or are occupied with a chore that can't be postponed. Explain to her why you can't play with her just now and when you will have time to. But remember, you should also be prepared to accept a no from your daughter if she does not wish to wear the red sweater or play the flute for her aunt. Making reasonable decisions for herself is her first step toward independence.

Set a good example

Living with children means that you must constantly ask yourself, 'What's really important to me?' If you can answer this question truthfully, if you know your core values and benchmarks, you can set clear priorities. This has an effect on your entire life, of course, but especially on your family life.

✦ ✦

What are your values?

✦ Which is more important to you, financial independence or good relationships with others?

✦ Do you pursue your own dreams or tend to adhere to social conventions?

✦ If you had to compile your own 'Ten Family Commandments', what would they be?

✦ What types of memories do you want to look back on when you are old?

✦ How would you like to be remembered by others, including your children?

✦ ✦

When my husband and I asked the participants at a seminar for couples to list their individual values and then compare them to their partners' values, there was quite a commotion. Many of the couples, some of whom had lived together for years, were surprised to discover how different their values were from their spouses'. And some differences fall into gender categories, or can be seen as 'typically male' or 'typically female' values.

Try not to criticize your partner if your values seem very different from his or hers. Instead, seek out the common values. Talk about what a particular value means to you and listen to your partner's response without judgment. (And if you both listed 'sense of humor' as a core value, you're already on track!)

Your children will judge you according to the example you set. You will not be credible if you are a chain-smoker and forbid your daughter from smoking. Nor will your advice be effective if you are a heavy drinker while insisting your daughter be a teetotaler. If you maintain a healthy lifestyle, you will be in a position to ask her to do the same. And if you enjoy playing with your children, you won't have to explain that joy in living is important to you; your children will know it!

Honesty is a quality that adults often demand from their children but don't demonstrate themselves. Examine your conscience. When have you lied, and in what situations have you disowned your convictions? Your children will want to speak to you about this one day.

In the wonderful book *Racism Explained to My Daughter,* author Tahar Ben Jelloun explains his values to his ten-year-old daughter, Meriem. Jelloun is a French writer of Moroccan descent who responds to his daughter's queries about racism at a time when many European nations were struggling to absorb (or not) citizens from their former colonies into their home populations. Jelloun examines the social, political, economic and psychological aspects of racism, touching on discrimination, religion, genetics, stereotyping, immigration and xenophobia. What he is really writing about are values. The book is easy to read and has been translated into more than a dozen languages. I strongly recommend it to all parents.

As long as you have children asking you questions, you will be challenged to reflect on your life and values. This is important in itself. Even if you hold a view on a particular issue that is completely different from your daughter's, she will remember the conversation the two of you had about it all her life—if you treat her opposing view with the same dignity and respect you expect her to give yours. And though she disagrees with you today, it doesn't mean she won't agree with you in the future.

Be a good role model

I repeat: children need role models. All children need adults of both genders to set meaningful examples for them. How do you speak about others?

- ✦ Is your boss 'an idiot'?

- ✦ Is your neighbor 'a jerk'?

- ✦ The driver in front of you 'a moron'?

- ✦ Your mother-in-law 'a witch'?

- ✦ Your ex-husband 'a slob'?

Observe and be honest with yourself and your children, and that's how they will be. A person who honestly expresses an opinion and stands up for their personal truth will always be respected.

✦ ✦ ✦ ✦ ✦ ✦ ✦ ✦ ✦ ✦ ✦ ✦ ✦ ✦ ✦ ✦ ✦ ✦ ✦ ✦

A role model in action

Before my husband and I had children, a friend dropped by for an unannounced visit with his daughter, Anne. (This was in the 1970s, before the punk rock movement had become widespread.) Anne arrived wearing shredded and 'graffitied' bluejeans and a provocative top. She had brightly dyed hair and probably wore a spiked dog-collar as well, I don't really remember. Her father treated her with dignity and respect throughout the visit, even though her appearance embarrassed him. I admired him tremendously for this. Without saying a word, his behavior toward his daughter clearly showed us all what love is.

✦ ✦ ✦ ✦ ✦ ✦ ✦ ✦ ✦ ✦ ✦ ✦ ✦ ✦ ✦ ✦ ✦ ✦ ✦ ✦

Eating with pleasure

Is eating a problematic family issue in your household? It certainly has become so in many American homes today. I find it remarkable (in the literal sense of the word) that in our overly mechanized culture, our most natural activities—eating, sleeping and sexuality—give us so much trouble. Shouldn't it make us stop and wonder why, when North America is groaning with a surplus of food, so many Americans consume an unhealthy diet and suffer from vitamin and mineral deficiencies? And why is it almost always girls (although more and more boys are being diagnosed with eating disorders) who diet obsessively or suffer with anorexia and bulimia? Why does a girl's body image at puberty become potentially life-threatening? And how can we as parents stand by our daughters and help them?

The best nourishment during the first months of life is mother's milk. It is the food that was designed for just us, and there is no equal alternative. From about the sixth month, children may also start eating some solids, carrot purée, for example. Once your daughter can sit in her own high chair with you at the table, you can start thinking about more comprehensive meals for her.

Food and mealtimes are an important part of every family's culture—who cooks, when and with which ingredients. Of course, you will have your own thoughts about this, but for the health of your children, a couple of points are worth bearing in mind. Processed baby food, precooked and presweetened 'instant' cereal and commercial fruit juices cannot compete with freshly cooked vegetables and cereal, or fresh-squeezed juice in terms of nutrients, however, not all fresh produce is equally nutritious. Have you considered buying organic fruits and veggies? What about organic meat, and free-range eggs? Freshly prepared cereal, vegetables and fruits,

organically grown and free of hormones, pesticides and other chemicals (whose long-term side effects are still not fully known) as well as genetic modification, are the best foods you can offer your family. This is the way the Earth intended you and your children to enjoy its bounty.

If you avoid giving your daughter sugar in the form of candies, pastries, sweetened cereal or sodas, for instance, you'll be doing a lot for her nutrition, and her teeth. Moreover, you'll also have a child who eats almost everything you put in front of her. The fussiest young eaters are often the children raised on processed packaged foods. If your daughter decides she doesn't like a certain type of vegetable, don't be too concerned. She will choose what she needs out of the range of things you offer her. And remember, a healthy child usually means happy parents!

Limiting sweets

If you do not stock unhealthy foods in your home, few problems can arise. When your child comes into contact with sweets (which are loaded with stabilizers, emulsifiers and other harmful substances) and she will (in school, perhaps, or at a friend's house), she will be less vulnerable to such offerings if you've already laid the foundation for good nutrition.

Parents often dispute this with me, claiming their child will go to a neighbor's or a friend's place for sweets and snacks. If she's still a toddler, she won't be going anywhere alone or left anywhere unsupervised. So there's no reason why you can't monitor what she eats. And if, when she's a bit older, she does eat sweets at her grandparents' house or when she's visiting with her friends, why make a drama out of it? You've done your best, and that's enough—because that's all you can do. Regardless, consuming less healthy meals or snacks once in while or on special occasions certainly won't harm her. As a rule, children raised on healthy food seldom choose to eat a lot of unhealthy food, even when it is available. If your child is in day care or when she goes to school, pack her lunch and snacks to ensure she gets the best nutrition you can provide.

✦ ✦ ✦ ✦ ✦ ✦ ✦ ✦ ✦ ✦ ✦ ✦ ✦ ✦ ✦ ✦ ✦ ✦ ✦ ✦

How much food is enough?

Don't be too worried that your daughter eats too little or too much. A healthy child eats exactly as much as she needs. However, this rule applies only if your child consumes a largely sugar-free diet. An excess of sugar leads to a desire for more and more sweet things, and from there it's a slippery slope to deficient nutrition.

✦ ✦ ✦ ✦ ✦ ✦ ✦ ✦ ✦ ✦ ✦ ✦ ✦ ✦ ✦ ✦ ✦ ✦ ✦ ✦

Food and power

If your daughter feels that she has the upper hand over you when it comes to her eating habits, make no mistake, she will exploit it. She may try something like, 'I'm not hungry,' even when you know she is, or 'I'm not eating *that!*' in the hope that you will immediately replace it with something else, like a canned or frozen meal (that's very high in sodium, flavor enhancers and preservatives) or maybe even a fast food meal (that's extremely high in sugars, fats and chemical additives). My advice is: don't. The result of this kind of exploitation is that frozen fish fingers, canned ravioli and heavily breaded, deep-fried chicken-in-a-bucket will eventually replace altogether the lightly grilled fresh fish, fresh pasta with steamed vegetables, and baked herb chicken you've been preparing for her.

She can help you cook

If you cook with pleasure, delight and love, your daughter will want to cook with you, so by all means encourage her to join you in the kitchen. As soon as she's old enough, let her help you decide what to prepare. Take her with you to the farmer's market and grocery store. Teach her about quality and freshness. Encourage her to choose produce and compare varieties. And, with plenty of supervision, allow her to participate in the actual meal preparation. Sensory experiences will increase her interest in cooking and her familiarity with the taste and texture of different foods.

In fact, during the first few years of life, children learn exclusively through sensory experience: listening, touching, tasting, smelling, examining, imitating and exploring things with their eyes, ears, noses, mouths, hands and their whole bodies. When you encourage your daughter to be part of such a marvelously sensory activity as food preparation, she will receive just the stimulation she needs. And if you think about it, preparing and consuming food engages all five senses—sight, sound, smell, touch and, of course, taste—like few other activities.

On the other hand, if your daughter experiences mainly canned or frozen or fast food, she might reasonably assume that corn comes from a can, fish from the freezer and the only kind of potato is a french fry!

Mealtime behavior

What happens during a meal is at least as important as your choice of food on the table. Meals should take place in a friendly, peaceful atmosphere, if at all possible. Anything else is unhealthy. Avoid criticizing your children or partner during mealtimes. Discussions over dinner are wonderful. Arguments are not. If problems need to be aired, go for a walk or go to another room and talk *after* the meal.

Discuss with your partner the kind of table manners you think are appropriate. Is your daughter allowed to leave the table when she has finished eating, or should she wait until everyone is finished? Can she play while she's eating, or is it reasonable to expect her to focus on her meal? Can she serve herself at a certain age, and if so, at what age? And must she eat everything on her plate?

There are no right or wrong answers to these questions. You will develop your own family culture by seeking answers

together and emphasizing the values that are important to you. In the past, for instance, a prayer (or 'grace') was usually said before meals, children weren't permitted to speak unless spoken to at the table, and everyone remained seated until all had finished eating. Today, for many families, practical considerations as well as values may have changed a little or a lot. These days there are some families that almost never sit down together for a meal, and saying grace may be reserved for holidays.

What are the values you would like to instill in your children? Are family mealtimes the most appropriate occasions for imparting your values? How do you want to shape your family culture in this respect? The moment your toddler joins you at the family table, she learns something, not only about food, but about where she belongs in the context of her family. What she learns is in your hands.

✦ ✦ ✦ ✦ ✦ ✦ ✦ ✦ ✦ ✦ ✦ ✦ ✦ ✦ ✦ ✦ ✦ ✦ ✦

Food, you and your daughter

✦ Meals with the whole family are fun.

✦ We should be grateful for our food; its plentifulness and variety should no be taken for granted.

✦ Healthy foods keep us well.

✦ Everyone can help with preparing meals.

✦ Children learn table manners most easily through example and praise, not through criticism or ridicule.

- ✦ Everyone's body belongs to them, therefore each person should choose from a healthy range of foods what and how much they eat.

- ✦ Fruits and vegetables should always be allowed as a snack.

✦ ✦ ✦ ✦ ✦ ✦ ✦ ✦ ✦ ✦ ✦ ✦ ✦ ✦ ✦ ✦ ✦ ✦

In a nutshell

- ✦ Accept and bond with the baby girl you actually have, not the one you might have been anticipating.

- ✦ You are doing your daughter a favor when you say no to her for a good reason.

- ✦ Good role models are vital for a girl's healthy emotional development.

- ✦ Your daughter is more likely to have positive, healthy attitudes toward eating if you start her off with fresh, natural foods and limited sweets.

Not tied to the apron strings! —Lisa

Everybody was busy in the kitchen when I announced that, instead of receiving presents for Mother's Day, I would not be cooking for three days over the weekend. I wanted a rest.

There was a sudden silence. Everyone looked at me, and then my two boys, aged 18 and 15, and their father turned to the youngest, Jesse, aged ten, and the only other female in the house, and said, 'Oh well, you'll be cooking for three days, then.'

Jesse threw herself onto the couch, put her feet up and announced, 'Sorry, I'm going to be a mother one day too, so I need to rest now. I can't do the cooking.'

On Mother's Day, Jesse gave me a card she had made that read:

Happy Mother's Day, Mom
Please don't die until I get married.
Love,
Jesse

I think she could see nothing but years of cooking for her brothers and father ahead of her!

Chapter 3

Her Early Years

In this chapter, we will look at important areas of a little girl's development and see how parents can help, encourage and support her. Again, the fundamental points here are that you should establish your values, you should stick to them and you should observe your daughter carefully and lovingly so that you will know what she needs.

Language development

One area in which little girls are usually ahead of little boys is in language development. According to one study, while girls can already speak three words at the age of ten months, boys of the same age can only manage one. By the age of eighteen months, half of all girls have a vocabulary of 56 words at their disposal, while half of all boys use only 28 words.

These differences also appear in their passive vocabulary (the vocabulary they understand but do not use themselves). At sixteen months, half of all girls understand 206 words, while half of all boys are getting by with 134 words. Boys will catch up to girls around the age of twenty months.

So overall, little girls have greater language fluency earlier in life because their left cerebral hemisphere is activated sooner, and this is where the language center lies. This brings us back to the differences between the male and female brain. Interestingly, parents tend to respond to this difference quite unconsciously, encouraging their daughter's speech habits more strongly than their son's. Another study showed that the number of words a parent directs to a child (the amount of communication they initiate) gives a fairly precise prediction of that child's intelligence, academic success and social skill. In fact, the more words directed at the child, the greater the child's ability in these areas.

Without a doubt, speaking stimulates the brain and assists in building neuron connections that are indispensable to a child's intelligence, creativity and adaptability. The language acquisition phase is therefore shaped by interaction, and this link becomes far more noticeable in years to come.

✦ ✦ ✦ ✦ ✦ ✦ ✦ ✦ ✦ ✦ ✦ ✦ ✦ ✦ ✦ ✦ ✦ ✦

One language or two?

If you are in a position to bring up your child bilingually, do it. Young children are able to acquire language very easily and quickly during the first few years of life—and it will never again be as easy for them. A second (or more) language ability not only contributes to your child's competency in her first language, it also has a positive effect on her overall intelligence.

✦ ✦ ✦ ✦ ✦ ✦ ✦ ✦ ✦ ✦ ✦ ✦ ✦ ✦ ✦ ✦ ✦ ✦

Various studies have shown that both preschool male and female teachers treat girls and boys differently. Girls are frequently supported in their language efforts; their natural talent in this area is fostered. But remember, language stimulation takes place by way of conversation, actually speaking to a child, not by playing cassettes, CDs or videos for them. Infants only improve their communication skills when they receive direct verbal interaction.

Language stimulation comes naturally to most parents: talking to your baby, explaining what you're doing, where you're going and why throughout the course of your day, singing to her, dancing with her and reading to her. If you do not do at least some of these things, your daughter's development may slow significantly or stall completely. This can happen, for instance, to children with parents that are hearing and speech impaired if another adult does not step in to provide routine verbal stimulation.

One of the most famous and extreme cases of learning deficiency is Kaspar Hauser, a foundling of unknown origin who surfaced in Nüremberg, Germany, in 1828. He was about sixteen years old but possessed many of the behavioral characteristics of a toddler: his vocabulary was rudimentary and pronunciation was primitive, he walked tentatively and stumbled easily, and he displayed a lack of modesty around women. Kaspar Hauser served as the model for a syndrome of the same name, which twentieth-century social psychologists characterized as a developmental disturbance. But you won't have to worry about anything as extreme as that—just keep talking to your kids!

What do sports, music and mud have to do with intelligence?

Just like baby boys, newborn girls are equipped with 100 billion nerve cells, of which only a small portion are already linked up to follow genetically specified circuits. The remainder of these nerve cells wait for a meaningful learning program. Via sensory perception and motor activity, the nervous system builds neurological pathways that lead to movements becoming first acquired and finally automated. We can observe these connections very clearly in infants.

Physical skills

At three months of age, a baby starts to watch her hands, and learns to guide them to her mouth. These are her first deliberate movements—hand to mouth. By frequent repetition, a neural pathway is formed; later, the movement is performed entirely unconsciously.

By the fifth month, a baby will learn to reach for an object purposefully. The sensations coming from an object (sight,

sound, smell, as examples) are transferred via nerve cells and electric impulses directly to her brain. Those impulses travel on from her brain to her muscles, enabling a deliberate movement. While your child is touching an object, she is noting the differences

between its form, texture, color and material and those
of other objects, and in this way she is developing abstract
concepts such as 'ball', 'Mommy' and 'car'.

During the toddler stage, all a child's learning
takes place through sensory perception. So give
your daughter various materials to feel: something smooth, something soft, something
round, something hard, something
heavy, something light, something
wet, something bumpy. Let her
play with mud, sand and water,
with pebbles and twigs, leaves and
grass. Let her experiment with
many kinds of movement: run-
ning, reaching, trotting, skipping, hopping, leaping, stretching,
sliding, standing on one foot, then the other, bowing forward
and twisting from side to side.

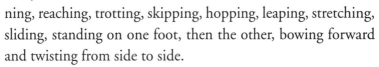

By the way, if your daughter plays the piano, all parts of her
brain will be activated. In fact, music, sports, painting and molding soft materials aren't just for fun; they also foster general intelligence. The assumption, of course, is that your daughter devotes
herself voluntarily and happily to these activities.

Goodbye diapers, hello potty

Most little girls get rid of their diapers quickly and easily. If she
is interested, take your daughter with you when you go to the
toilet. Show her what you do there and offer her the chance to
copy you with the help of a child-sized toilet seat or potty chair.

I recommend letting her play outdoors without a diaper
during the hot summer months, so that she will notice when she

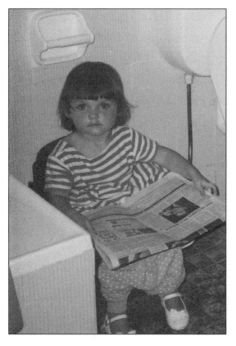

urinates. It's not a good idea to pressure her. And punishment almost always prolongs the process. Simply be appreciative with every success, but there's no need to be overly dramatic. In fact, I usually suggest to parents that they not pay the whole operation too much attention. Sooner or later, every child is toilet-trained.

I know of only a few cases when the 'take off the diaper' strategy was unsuccessful. Even if the living room carpet has to be cleaned afterwards, I believe it's worth trying this natural approach. Once in a while, there will be accidents. However, in most cases deliberate refusal is due to fear. For example, one little girl, Marie, thought she was losing part of her body when she saw her excretions. Her mother was not able to convince her otherwise, and Marie screamed her little head off and demanded a diaper each time she had to go. But after some calming explanations and some adult observations of Marie going to the toilet—and vice versa—the problem was soon solved.

✦ ✦ ✦ ✦ ✦ ✦ ✦ ✦ ✦ ✦ ✦ ✦ ✦ ✦ ✦ ✦ ✦ ✦

When toilet-training doesn't seem to be working

Parents should be reassured about one thing: If a child is having problems getting rid of her diapers, it is not because her parents have done something wrong. Rather, it is because she misunderstands what is expected of her or it's because she is worried or frightened about what's going on. Patience, sympathy and understanding are what she needs during this time. Punishment, disdain or ridicule will only lead to an intensification of the problem, which will make it even more difficult to find a solution.

✦ ✦ ✦ ✦ ✦ ✦ ✦ ✦ ✦ ✦ ✦ ✦ ✦ ✦ ✦ ✦ ✦ ✦

In this context, I'd like to put in a word for sheepskin. If you place a fluffy sheepskin in your daughter's bed, above the sheet, it doesn't just keep her warm; it also helps her feel safe. And if she does wet the bed at night, the bed linens and mattress are protected. Then, simply dry the sheepskin in the sun, and there will be hardly any odor.

Girls learn earlier

Author Susan Gilbert maintains that one of the main differences between boys and girls is that girls learn more easily from their mistakes. Do you agree? American psychologist Eleanor Maccoby observed one-year-old boys and girls in a doctor's waiting room. While the boys often reached for objects their parents had forbidden them to touch, the girls generally stuck to the rules. Were the girls simply better behaved?

There is a classic experiment that tests the memory skills and impulse control of eight-month-old crawling children. An object is hidden in one place in a room, and the child is allowed to find it; then, while the child is watching, the object is retrieved and placed somewhere else in the room. Most children will initially look where it was hidden the first time. Either they have forgotten that it has been moved to a new location or they cannot resist the impulse to look for it where they had previously found it. In one study, the older the children were, the better both girls and boys became at this experiment, however, girls made faster progress.

The situation is similar with toilet hygiene. Most parents notice that girls control their bladders earlier than boys. One investigation found that among two-and-a-half-year-olds, 30 percent of girls and only 15 percent of boys were toilet-trained. By the age of three, 70 percent of girls had managed it, but only half the boys had. Maccoby traces this difference back to the variation in degree of brain maturity in boys and girls of the same age. Of course, you will know about exceptions to these generalizations.

All in all, girls generally seem to be able to control themselves more reliably than boys. This is also apparent in terms of tantrums, which are normal for one- and two-year-old children. From the age of three, however, girls tend to have fewer tantrums than boys. They also tend to adjust to preschool life more smoothly than boys.

Sexual curiosity

While a little boy's penis is clearly visible and is, quite early on, discovered to be a source of physical pleasure for its owner, it's not so straightforward with girls. Parents sometimes forget that their daughter also experiences sexual urges. So when a little girl touches her genitals, an adult may feel compelled to scold her and shame her and will often forbid any further touching.

The visible parts of the female sexual organs are designated as the labia (lips). In German they are called *Schamlippen,* which

literally means 'shame lips'. Other words that represent the concepts of coyness, shamelessness, disgrace, and defilement—all of which have a negative connotation—derive etymologically from the root word 'shame' in the German language. Fortunately, other cultures deal with female genitalia much more respectfully: in Chinese, for example, they are known as the 'heavenly gate', a much more appropriate and accurate description!

What lies protected, hidden behind this heavenly gate is the most precious female property: the clitoris. The clitoris, with 8,000 nerve fibers, is more sensitive than any other female body part and far more sensitive than the penis. And its sole function is to give women pleasure—from youth to old age!

✦ ✦ ✦ ✦ ✦ ✦ ✦ ✦ ✦ ✦ ✦ ✦ ✦ ✦ ✦ ✦ ✦ ✦ ✦ ✦

The center of pleasure

American journalist and author Natalie Angier writes, 'It's only in the clitoris that we see a sexual organ that is so exclusively dedicated to its function and task that it doesn't need any props or aids whatsoever. For this reason, perhaps it's clever that the clitoris normally stays hidden in the labia folds. In a way it's a private joke, a divine secret, a Pandora's box that doesn't contain a single bad thing, but for all that is brimful of pleasure.'

✦ ✦ ✦ ✦ ✦ ✦ ✦ ✦ ✦ ✦ ✦ ✦ ✦ ✦ ✦ ✦ ✦ ✦ ✦ ✦

Little girls usually discover this anatomical wonder early, all by themselves, and we should simply let them do so. A girl who is allowed to explore her own body in her own time and in a casual way is more likely to feel at ease with herself and less likely to have troubling body image issues.

✦ ✦ ✦ ✦ ✦ ✦ ✦ ✦ ✦ ✦ ✦ ✦ ✦ ✦ ✦ ✦ ✦ ✦ ✦

Physical exploration

Men and boys can look at and understand their sexual organs with ease. For girls, however, self-exploration is a little more challenging. In fact, many adult women don't know what they look like 'down there' unless they've examined themselves with the help of a mirror. Your daughter might want to do the same. And she may not. If she is curious, show her where urine comes out, what the clitoris is and which opening she came from when she was born.

✦ ✦ ✦ ✦ ✦ ✦ ✦ ✦ ✦ ✦ ✦ ✦ ✦ ✦ ✦ ✦ ✦ ✦ ✦

Every human body is a miracle, and our daughters should know this about themselves. And what distinguishes a woman's body from a man's is its capacity to carry new life, to bear and nourish a child.

Fathers and daughters—what's okay?

Fathers may feel uncertain about how to behave physically around their young daughters, because of the possibility of false accusations of sexual impropriety. What can a father do safely with his little girl and what is forbidden? There is a very simple rule of thumb that I feel always applies to every parent/child relationship: *Maintain the generation gap at all times.* As an adult, whether you are a father or a mother, it is your duty and responsibility to set limits. As a father, you may be as tender toward your daughter as you wish to be—and as she wishes you to be. Should you become sexually aroused when playing, which can happen, it is your job as a father to draw the line and end the game. Children's sexuality and adult sexuality must not be blended. A child can't be expected to understand the difference—that's a parent's job. Your daughter is depending on you to know what is appropriate. You, as the adult, *always* bear responsibility for the child.

Many little girls learn how to flirt to perfection. Their charm is irresistible. This is exactly why fathers must set clear boundaries, in line with their responsibility. Don't allow your daughter to wrap you around her little finger, but don't reject her abruptly, either, when she goes too far. Tell her clearly what is okay and what is *not* okay with you. Further explanations aren't necessary.

✦ ✦ ✦ ✦ ✦ ✦ ✦ ✦ ✦ ✦ ✦ ✦ ✦ ✦ ✦ ✦ ✦ ✦

An awkward situation between mother and son

A mother told me recently that when her little boy was six, he had asked her, in the bathtub one day, 'Mummy, will we fuck?' Once she got over her shock and confusion, she asked what he meant, and he explained it to her expertly: to poke his penis into her vagina. She did not bathe with him again. When she told me this, ten years had passed since the incident. 'I should have answered him quite calmly at the time, "No, we don't do that. That is something I only do with your father."'

✦ ✦ ✦ ✦ ✦ ✦ ✦ ✦ ✦ ✦ ✦ ✦ ✦ ✦ ✦ ✦ ✦ ✦

Remember, **your children are not in this world to give *you* pleasure.**

And I'm not just talking about sexual pleasure. One young woman told me that when she was a child her father had insisted she dance for him. He thought her dancing was beautiful—but she didn't. Eventually, she quit dancing altogether because her associations with it had become so oppressive. Another woman I know was forced to cuddle with her father in a certain position she didn't enjoy and didn't feel comfortable in. Expressing physical affection became quite difficult for her as an adult.

Clearly, when we try to make our children do things they instinctively don't want to do, but acquiesce to for our gratification, we are teaching them to disregard they're inner guidance and better judgment—qualities most children possess innately. Needless to say, this is not a good message to send.

Each of us, young and old, craves tenderness and affection, and you can't lavish too much of either on a child. But we, as parents, must know where our boundaries are and stay within them—your daughter is counting on it.

Do you want to return to work?

Australia and New Zealand are countries where working parents, especially mothers, have it anything but easy. Often when a woman takes on a position of responsibility at her job, she will likely be asked, 'How will this affect your children?' But a man in the same situation would not be asked this. Even after more than thirty years of women's liberation, our society still works this way. I will address the following section to mothers, although this does not mean I assume dads won't take time off from work, or don't want to do so.

Regardless of the child-care arrangements and restrictions that exist where you live and work, we should first ask, is it sensible, practical, essential to go to work if you're a mother with a child under the age of five? There are several things to consider. Assuming you enjoyed some time off for maternity leave from your job, do you actually want to go back to work again? Do you have to return to work for financial reasons? Is there any possibility that you don't want to be a stay-at-home mom because other people wouldn't value or respect that choice? Or could it be because *you* don't value or respect that choice? Do you get a lot of pleasure from your career? Or would you honestly rather be at home with your child? And if you do want to return to your job again, what sort of hours would suit you and your new family?

First, recall that happy parents are more likely to have happy children. If you're dissatisfied as a mother, you will impart these feelings to your child. Are you someone who loves to go to her job? If you give up your career and stay home with your daughter, will you feel trapped and resentful? Then you must acknowledge this and do something about it. There's no shame in being honest with yourself and your family. If this is how you feel, then it makes much more sense to look for a qualified nanny/caregiver or day-care situation for your daughter.

It is definitely not natural (in any sense of the word) for a mother to spend hours and hours each day feeling isolated with her baby at home. In centuries past, women tended to band together to care for their children in groups. This not only gave children many opportunities for social learning experiences, it also gave each mother extra pairs of hands, as well as more time for other chores in addition to feeding and watching the little ones. There was always someone to comfort a child and play with her; and in the case of a crisis, Mother was always nearby and help was at hand.

In Australia and New Zealand, more and more single women are raising children alone. Most of them have to be working mothers, whether they want to or not, simply to manage financially. Whether you go to a job because you wish to or because you have to, your working life will not harm your daughter if you find a care-giver or day-care situation where she receives loving, consistent and conscientious care.

Child-care options

If you think (or know) that you will need child-care at some point in the future, you may need to put your name down at a number of day-care centers early on. These days, that might mean before your baby is born! But whenever you decide you're ready to start researching child-care facilities, make a list of all the qualities you feel are essential before you visit them, then look carefully to be sure your expectations are met. Some general issues to consider:

✦ What kind of impression do the children at the facility make on you? Do they seem happy and busy? Or cranky or unattended?

✦ How do staff members interact with the children? How would you imagine them interacting with your child?

✦ Is the facility clean, well-ventilated and attractive? Can you imagine yourself spending much of the day there?

✦ What nutritional choices will be are offered?

✦ What sort of medical care is available on site?

If you decide against using a commercial day-care center, family day care, in which a relatively small number of children (say, five or six) are cared for in a private home, is another option. A reliable babysitter in your own home or a live-in or part-time nanny are alternatives to consider. Of course, these options are more expensive. However, if you are honest, I think you'll agree that a well-qualified mother-substitute is worth a decent salary.

But before you employ someone, watch how she interacts with your daughter and how your daughter responds to her. If at all possible, give them some time to get to know each other. When the two of them have established a stable relationship, comparable to a family member, then you can go to work with confidence and a clear conscience.

Of course, it would be wonderful if you have family members who could step in and look after your daughter—grandmothers, mothers-in-law, aunties—are often ideal, if they're available. And, of course, your daughter's father could look after her in your absence. However, there are several factors that combine to make this difficult:

✦ Many fathers simply do not wish to give up, or even take a leave of absence from, their jobs in order to stay home with their children.

✦ A part-time job may not be available for the dad who would be happy to reduce his working hours in favor of child-raising.

✦ Most men earn more money than their female partners, so many families cannot afford the reduction in income.

In many cases, a family's financial situation is such that none of these possibilities can realistically even be considered. This is a great pity, because it perpetuates the trend of the 'fatherless society'. Another difficulty that many parents face today is that they may only see each other for a few hours each day, which means they must make a conscious effort not to let their own relationship suffer.

Many women would gladly work from home part-time or full-time in order to have more time with their kids. And in some occupations, this is already possible. This can be a desirable option *if* you are able to determine (and control) how much time you spend on work and how much time is devoted to your child. However, if you can't establish and adhere to such limits, first you, then your daughter and finally your job, will suffer, and then the whole family could face serious consequences. So, what sounds like the perfect solution to the child-care dilemma can produce its own special set of problems.

Choosing to stay home

If you are a woman who is willingly interrupting your career for a while in order to raise your family full time, stick to your guns and enjoy this period of your life! You'll find there are lots of ways to celebrate being with your daughter: you can cook for her, make her toys, sew her clothes, decorate her room, write stories and poems for her and illustrate them with your paintings and drawings, take photographs and videos of her, and consider devoting some time to a hobby you find especially fulfilling and bring your baby daughter with you. As she gets older, you can do all these activities with her.

Make a point of introducing yourself to other mothers with little girls in your building, neighborhood or town. Share your experiences, observations and insights with them as your kids play and progress together. These are friendships that can last a lifetime—between mother and mother and daughter and daughter.

Don't let yourself be talked into believing that you're lazy for leaving your job or old-fashioned for wanting to be with your kids. Countless other women are doing exactly the same as you, and their children are the better for it!

It is simply wonderful to live with a child! Just listen to Steve Biddulph, the well-known Australian family therapist, who has spoken out vehemently against strangers looking after our children. His credo is, 'Why did you have the child if you are just going to have her looked after by strangers? Are we living in a cuckoo society where you place your young in someone else's nest?'

Money isn't the only factor

Because our standard of living is determined largely by our financial obligations, it would be unfair to blame *all* the problems of children and families on the fact that many mothers have to work. (By the way, a materialistic lifestyle is by no means without alternatives, and we all bear responsibility for our choices, whether we have children or not.) Abuse and neglect of a child can certainly occur even when the mother is at home all the time. So we must ask ourselves what kind of culture have we created that drives a parent to such extremes? (One of the child-care options outlined above might be the salvation of many such children.)

On the other hand, you as parents carry the seed of a new culture within you. Your children are your future. Which are the skills they will need? And upon what sort of a foundation will they best develop these skills?

I would like to make a suggestion here: If your financial situation allows it, make the decision about whether or not to go back to work by following your heart. Think about how you would organize your life, if you could, to derive the maximum satisfaction from it. What would this life look like? Leave all the arguments to one side and just contemplate this imaginary, ideal life. Write down all the elements that would comprise such a life, or draw a diagram of it if that feels more natural to you. Shift yourself mentally into this life. How does feel? How does it work? Is it what you want?

Now sit down with whomever you wish to involve in this decision (parents, partner, a sibling, a best friend) and discuss this ideal life, and try to work out how to make it happen, step by step. Barbara Sher's wonderful book, *Wishcraft*, (see References on page 194) may help you with this.

✦ ✦ ✦ ✦ ✦ ✦ ✦ ✦ ✦ ✦ ✦ ✦ ✦ ✦ ✦ ✦ ✦ ✦ ✦

My personal vision

I dream of conquering isolation by living a more communal life. In this dream, young families live very close together and support one another. Children play together, and parents are freed from the isolation of the nuclear family. The tasks around the home and grounds are taken care of cooperatively. Some mothers and fathers work outside this community, while others stay within it to look after the children. Some singles and couples without children also belong to this extended family group, and take on the tasks they enjoy. There are surrogate grandparents and godparents. Conflicts are constructively solved, and each child has several role models, thereby learning about various lifestyles and value systems. Every person contributes his or her own skills and receives help whenever it is needed. Humanity is the hallmark of this scenario.

✦ ✦ ✦ ✦ ✦ ✦ ✦ ✦ ✦ ✦ ✦ ✦ ✦ ✦ ✦ ✦ ✦ ✦ ✦

In a nutshell

✦ As babies and toddlers, girls develop faster than boys physically, emotionally and intellectually.

✦ Let your daughter explore her body without restriction, criticism or judgment.

✦ With fathers and daughters, as with parents and children in general, it is vital to 'keep the generation gap' at all times.

✦ If you're considering whether or when to return to work, bear in mind that happy parents are more likely to have happy children.

Up close and too personal—Mindy

My daughter, Katie, and I were at the Chiang Mai Zoo, in northern Thailand, peering over the cement wall into the elephant enclosure. Katie was about two years old, and I was holding her in my right arm, waving a banana with my left hand at the elephant inside. The elephant strolled over to the wall. Unlike Western zoos, where there's no feeding of the animals, at the Chiang Mai Zoo vendors sell bags of peanuts and stalks of bananas especially for that purpose.

(continued)

I gave her (I'm certain it was a female) a banana, which she delicately inserted into the envelope of her mouth. Then her trunk reached across the wall for more. I had more, but first I wanted to check out that extraordinary trunk. It was like a huge tentacle, with little bristly hairs, and lots and lots of wrinkles. I stroked it. I looked into the long vacuum tube of its opening. I breathed into her trunk, a breezy little tickle up her nose from me to her, and I tickled the outside of it a bit, too, marveling at how elastic and strong it seemed, and wondering how long my new friend would accept my playfulness.

Not very long at all, as it turned out. Suddenly the trunk I'd been tickling reached out and wrapped its coiled strength around my left wrist. I waited a moment, then tried to draw my hand back. The elephant exerted her mighty pull precisely the same amount in her direction, with (and I could feel the vast energy behind it) plenty of power in reserve. I stood there a moment thinking, 'I am in the complete grip of an immense force of nature, who is annoyed with me.' Then I met Katie's gaze of quiet alarm. The elephant looked at Katie, too. I wonder if she remembered being a mother, imperfect as we all are. She released me.

'Give the elephant another banana?' Katie asked.

'Okay.' I gave her the whole bunch.

Chapter 4

Her Emotional World

I would now like to shift the focus to the internal world of your daughter, and especially to the vital and dynamic world of her emotions. First, let's look at how to help her feel good about herself, and how she can safeguard her self-esteem.

The importance of self-esteem

High self-esteem is the best protection you can give your daughter. High self-esteem means she will consider herself to be an important and valuable participant in the world, regardless of her appearance, abilities or performance. If she knows she is irreplaceable, she will speak up for herself, defend her rights and her body. Any woman can become the victim of a violent act, of course, but in the light of the research

cited by Nicky Marone (see page 61), the odds are dramatically reduced among women with high self-esteem.

When I was a child, my friends and I often played the game, 'Who's afraid of the big bad wolf?' One group would stand in a row and call out the question.

'No one!' the other group would roar back, lined up facing them.

'And if he comes?'

'Then he just comes!'

At this point, you had to run—the aim was to get through the other team's line without being caught. Sadly, this game has gone out of fashion, but wherever girls played it, they made the same exciting discovery: that you can take a risk, emerge victorious and get to your destination safely. If your daughter plays a team sport, she will experience something similar.

Allow your daughter to express all her feelings, even the negative ones like jealousy, frustration and rage. Aggression is not all bad, because we can use it to stand up for ourselves in general, and assert ourselves in specific situations. Today, it is perfectly acceptable to 'feel' our feelings—to actually experience and express our emotions. In earlier times, girls were rarely allowed to defend themselves or to be loud or behave passionately. This was very detrimental to women, because we learned that expressing emotions is essential for good health. Teach your daughter that she can say 'no' and that she has the right to decide how and when to use her body. This concept extends even to apparently 'minor' things, like not persistently demanding a kiss from her if she is not so inclined; and not making her sit on your lap when she doesn't want to.

✦ ✦ ✦ ✦ ✦ ✦ ✦ ✦ ✦ ✦ ✦ ✦ ✦ ✦ ✦ ✦ ✦

Being overprotective vs. being safe

Many parents insist on driving their children not only to and from school, but to and from every event and activity as well. They do so largely out of fear that their daughter (or son) could be victimized or taken by a kidnapper or sex offender. While this is perfectly understandable and, in many cases, a wise and necessary precaution, there may be some locations and occasions when your kids could quite safely walk or take public transport to their destination. The reality is that we can't protect our daughters from every source of risk in the world. Rather, we need to prepare them to go out into the world without supervision but armed with self-confidence, self-esteem and good sense. And one way we can do this is to teach them to scream, defend themselves and run. Our inhibitions about making noise, or 'making a scene' or offending someone can sometimes put us in greater danger than would otherwise exist.

To illustrate this point, psychologist and author Nicky Marone quotes a study in which researchers filmed ordinary pedestrians in New York City as they strolled along a Manhattan street. The film was shown to a group of ex-offenders all of whom had served time in prison for violent street crimes. They were asked to identify which people in the film were worth considering as victims. The results were unequivocal: the same people were selected over and over. Each potential victim stood out because of his or her inhibited body language, which indicated fragility, uncertainty and a general lack of self-confidence.

✦ ✦ ✦ ✦ ✦ ✦ ✦ ✦ ✦ ✦ ✦ ✦ ✦ ✦ ✦ ✦ ✦ ✦ ✦

The best way you can protect your daughter from fear, and from danger, is to ensure that she has good self-esteem. There are many ways to do this, and you can start from the moment she is born.

Fathers and self-esteem

A father can do a lot for his little girl's self-esteem by loving her, respecting her *and* accepting her. Mind you, these feelings must be expressed not only in words but also in your actions. Love,

respect and acceptance must be demonstrated by your behavior with her, as words mean little when they are not supported by deeds. The father who tells his daughter 'you're the best at everything' but five minutes later demands why she didn't make the 'easy goal' in a soccer game, or the father who insists 'you're the prettiest girl in the world' but scolds her about her weight at breakfast, may discover he has a mistrustful young woman under his roof.

Spend quality time with your daughter. Give her the recognition she deserves for what she has achieved, rather than empty compliments for super-ficial things. Praise her for her values: her gentleness with animals and her will-ingness to share toys with her brother. Applaud her persistence at new and challenging tasks, like tying her shoes or practicing at the piano. Teach her the things that only you, her father, can teach her. It doesn't matter what your particular skills are: Whatever skills you have, I assure you, your daughter will value and use them!

✦ ✦ ✦ ✦ ✦ ✦ ✦ ✦ ✦ ✦ ✦ ✦ ✦ ✦ ✦ ✦ ✦

My father

I had a very loving father, so I can tell you how I felt his love. He kept several of my childhood drawings and looked after them as if they were priceless art treasures. He often took me for walks and would hold my hand;

I can still feel that beautiful sensation today. He read me enchanting fairy tales and thrilling adventure stories, and they are still with me. He taught me about animals and plants, and I still remember much of what he said. He allowed my little brother and me to stay quietly in his study while he sat at his desk working, which made us feel so important. Sometimes, he sang to us, and I can still hear him in my mind today.

When I got older, he tried helping me with math homework, but in vain, I'm afraid. He typed up my school compositions and kept them carefully stored away in a desk drawer. When he met with my teachers, he talked with them for as long as was necessary. He was always ready to answer my questions, or to look up the answer if he didn't know it. He tried to protect me from harm and always gave me his opinion—often, unasked. I didn't always want to hear what he had to say, and sometimes I rolled my eyes with impatience. Today, I know that in most things he was right.

✦ ✦ ✦ ✦ ✦ ✦ ✦ ✦ ✦ ✦ ✦ ✦ ✦ ✦ ✦ ✦ ✦ ✦

Encourage her early and often

Opportunities to promote and reinforce your daughter's self-esteem exist even when she is a toddler. It isn't always necessary to hurry to her aid if things go wrong. Leave it to her to find solutions by herself, and possibly to 'fail' and try again. When she's stacking building blocks, for example, the tower will topple if it gets too high and is not stable from below. Eventually, through trial and error, your daughter will learn how to build a tower that won't fall down. (And playing with building blocks will foster her spatial imagination.) It's also completely normal for a toddler to fall over when she is learning to walk. And it's okay to let her fall (on carpeting or grass) and stand up again, and fall again, as many times as it takes. These experiences are indispensable if a little girl is to learn to navigate through the world on her own some day.

Observe your daughter: What interests her? What does she enjoy? What is she good at? Support her in what gives her pleasure *and* urge her to try new things. Don't worry, you won't make a daredevil out of a naturally reserved child. And your efforts at transforming a daredevil into a child that is quiet and reserved will be equally doomed to failure.

While she is small, your daughter will feel valued when you look after her in a consistent way: Carry her often and touch her tenderly; when you speak to her, be sure to listen to her and take her needs seriously. A child develops self-esteem when she feels the unconditional love of her parents, a love that is grounded in her worth as a unique human being, not on her appearance or abilities. In this way, your daughter's self-esteem will grow even when she fails at something, or when she doesn't perform as well as she was expected to, or when she doesn't look the way you hoped she would. Self-esteem will grow and bloom as long as she senses 'My parents love me just the way I am!'

How does a child know that she is loved by her parents? By having the experience that her parents enjoy looking after her, that they have time for her, by showing interest in what she does, and expressing their affection. It's really quite simple. Treat your child with respect and dignity. When your daughter draws her first line, praise her. Your joy is all the incentive she needs to continue drawing. Every episode of praise and support is a step forward toward the development of confidence, self-esteem, and ultimately, independence.

✦ ✦

Fathers, daughters and play

In one study, a group of fathers was asked to complete a jigsaw puzzle with their sons and daughters. When the little boys had tantrums because they got frustrated with the puzzle, the fathers tended to ignore the tantrum and continue working on the puzzle. But if the girls started to cry, they were immediately comforted by their daddies with statements like, 'It doesn't matter, darling.' Or 'Let me help you, sweetie.'

If a little girl has this kind of experience often enough, she may tend to make less of an effort with things. Some girls will even deliberately behave as if they are helpless. By trying to make it easier for girls, and not letting them work out their problems for them-selves, we are actually undermining rather than enhanc-ing their self-esteem. Do with your daughter what you would do with your son: let her try to figure out on her own how the puzzle pieces fit together. She will master it sooner or later, and as a result, she will make you almost as proud of her as she is proud of herself!

✦ ✦

Let her imagine and create

Criticism, ignorance, negative or derogatory and sarcastic comments—all are harmful to children. Attacks on your daughter's self-esteem, especially when it comes from adults, and even teachers, can have disastrous long-term consequences. In this context, I'd like to stress that television may harm small children.

First and foremost, passive television viewing keeps kids from doing something active outdoors, which is so essential to their physical *and* mental growth and development. Second, a flood of sights and sounds from the television does little to stimulate a child's imagination. In fact, this onslaught of imagery may actually reduce their ability to fantasize. And an active imagination is the basis of all creative intelligence.

The more creatively active we are, the more accomplished and worthy we feel. When nurtured in childhood, this feeling never leaves us and remains with us throughout our lives. That's one reason why it's a good idea not to give a child too many fully assembled playthings; it's important for her to create, construct and compete some things herself. The Swedish author Astrid Lindgren wrote a very beautiful story about this, called *The Princess Who Did Not Want to Play,* in which a pampered princess becomes terribly bored in her castle. Although surrounded by toys, she doesn't know how to play. When Maja, a child with a lively imagination, arrives with a simple wooden doll, she initiates a wonderful playtime and opens the Princess's mind to the world of make-believe.

Creative play has been recognized as such an important component to childhood development that a number of preschools are starting to initiate 'toy-free' days. Teachers know that children, if left to their own devices, will come up with wonderful ideas for toys and games all by themselves, and will readily utilize furniture, paper, boxes and packing materials, old clothes, and natural materials like sand, water, wood and stones.

Children who are able to occupy and entertain themselves with very little, and who learn that they can affect the course of events through their own choices and actions, become self-confident, emotionally strong adults. Such self-assured people are far less likely to be defenseless victims of external circumstances later in life.

Dealing with fear

Every child feels fear sometimes. But whereas adult men are discouraged from showing fear or anxiety or uncertainty, women, and especially girls, are allowed and in some cases even encouraged to do so. This is probably why your daughter is more likely to admit to being afraid than your son is.

Jerome Kagan, Professor of Psychology at Harvard University, examined the issue of fear among boys and girls in a longitudinal study (that is, a study of one group of children over a period of

years) and found that even as toddlers, girls behave more fearfully than boys. As infants, both genders reacted in the same way to new, unknown stimuli such as a strong odor or a brightly colored hanging mobile. Each gender was curious, but not afraid. But by the age of fourteen months, sharply defined differences in response had already emerged. The more fearful children—mainly girls—exhibited increased heart rate, produced more stress hormones in their blood, and showed more tension in their faces with enlarged pupils and fretful expressions. These signs indicate activity in the amygdala, an almond-shaped nucleus in the brain's limbic system, which registers and triggers fear responses. Because androgens (male hormones) have a calming effect on the nerve cells in the amygdala, boys usually show less fear.

But Kagan also believes that, biological differences notwithstanding, excessive fear in girls is connected to overprotective care they might receive from parents, teachers and other adults. If you allow your daughter to have normal experiences, which include accidents like falling over or slipping, she will learn to deal with such mishaps as a matter of course. However, 'protecting' her from such ordinary daily events will only serve to keep her dependent and anxious. It has been observed that parents often encourage their young daughters to give up on certain tasks or cease certain activities that may be too 'dangerous' or 'unsuitable' for girls. Boys, on the other hand, are usually told the opposite and are routinely encouraged to persevere 'no matter what' and 'never back down' or 'never give up' regardless of the outcome.

Accepting feelings

Anger is an emotion everyone knows, and it has many important functions. Among other things, it helps us take responsibility for ourselves and it gives us courage. Studies show that it is unwise and unhealthy to suppress anger. Sooner or later, suppressed anger will manifest in a physical way. It may emerge as illness, or as fear.

Fear, too (and this cannot be emphasized enough) is, like every other emotion, both meaningful and useful. Fear keeps us safe by warning us to watch out for ourselves, by helping us recognize and come to terms with the reality of a risky situation. Fear helps us prepare for difficult or unknown circumstances. Instead of allowing ourselves to be overwhelmed by fear and paralyzed into helplessness, we can use it to galvanize us into action. Fear can be a source of energy that can help us solve a problem or cope with a situation or handle a task.

✦ ✦ ✦ ✦ ✦ ✦ ✦ ✦ ✦ ✦ ✦ ✦ ✦ ✦ ✦ ✦ ✦ ✦

Managing new situations

Take a visit to the dentist, for example. It is completely normal for a child to be frightened of this new and potentially scary situation. Say to your daughter, 'I understand that you're afraid. When we go someplace different or try something new, we don't know what to expect, so it's okay to be a little nervous or anxious about it. And that's exactly why you *should* try it. Next time, we'll know what to expect and it won't seem so scary.' Explain to her that fear helps us get ready for a new situation: 'I'm afraid, but I'm going to do it anyway.' That's a very important sentence, because it will remind her of her own strength. Talk about what will happen at the dentist's office. Once the dentist visit is successfully completed, your child will feel proud of herself: 'It's over. I did it! I was scared, but I went anyway! And it wasn't so bad.' That's an incredible feeling!

✦ ✦ ✦ ✦ ✦ ✦ ✦ ✦ ✦ ✦ ✦ ✦ ✦ ✦ ✦ ✦ ✦ ✦

The more often your daughter has the positive experience of overcoming her anxiety, the easier it will be the next time, and the time after that. Remind her that the first time she got on her bike she was scared, but she learned how to ride it and now she loves it. Remind her that she used to be frightened of water, but now she loves swimming and diving. Remind her how she didn't want to go to school, but now she can't wait to get there!

Reducing fear

As well as dealing with specific situations as they come up, there are several ways you can help your daughter reduce her fear overall:

✦ **Encourage your daughter's physical skills.** By exploring her physical strengths, she will also learn to control her body, and this in turn will give her a sense of increased physical confidence, which in turn reduces fear (see page 157). You can start early with simple games which fathers, in particular, tend to play with their daughters. For example, many dads lift their daughters high over their heads and 'fly' them around the room or around the garden. Baby swim classes not only keep kids safe at the beach and around the pool, it also conditions very young bodies. Ballet lessons and gymnastics classes from an early age are great for developing coordination, balance, strength, grace and agility. (But be careful here not to make comparisons between your daughter and her siblings or friends!) Discover what your daughter enjoys and encourage her to extend her skills.

✦ **Singing is also a fun way to counter fear.** (We don't say 'Whistle when you're in the dark' for nothing!) If

you sing often with your daughter, not only will this enhance her memory skills, she'll also build up a repertoire of songs that may be a source of comfort and confidence to her. There are even CDs and cassette recordings available to help children cope with fear. Don't leave your daughter alone to play these. The idea is to enjoy them with her, singing aloud together. Every time your daughter feels a sense of achievement, with you to cheer her on, she is increasing her confidence and reducing her fear.

✦ **Relaxation exercises are also a proven means for coping with fear.** A person who knows how to make herself relax can handle most frightening situations with confidence. Include some fantasy journeys and relaxation exercises during your bedtime storytelling. This will give your daughter a real treasure for her journey through life. You'll find ideas for appropriate stories in any library, as there are many books available filled with stories about children who have mastered their fears.

✦ ✦ ✦ ✦ ✦ ✦ ✦ ✦ ✦ ✦ ✦ ✦ ✦ ✦ ✦ ✦ ✦ ✦ ✦ ✦

Reducing fear through fantasy

Regardless of religious beliefs, many children find the idea of a guardian angel—a kind and gentle celestial being who comes down to Earth and always watches over them—very comforting. An angel or guardian spirit can be used to help soothe and reduce anxiety in your daughter, especially as she is drifting off to sleep at night.

Journey to your guardian angel

Make yourself quite comfortable ... and feel how your breath is rising and falling, all by itself ... feel your feet ... your legs ... your hips ... and your stomach ... Let your stomach go soft and feel how it moves with your breath…Feel your back…your chest…your shoulders… And then imagine that you can send your breath down through both of your arms when you exhale, so that it exits through your fingertips (longer pause)… Now feel your neck, your head…your chin…your upper and lower jaw are not touching…your tongue is lying gently on the roof of your mouth…your cheeks are soft and relaxed… And now imagine that the next breath you draw goes right through your body, so that it leaves through your toes… and with your next exhaled breath, imagine that the breath sprays out of the top of your head like a whale's… And now imagine that your breath has turned a beautiful color… so that sooner or later you are being wrapped up in a sphere of soft colored light… And you're lying there safe and sound… Now you can go on a journey in your sphere…to the stars or to the moon… and sooner or later you'll meet a guardian angel… Perhaps you'll see her or perhaps you'll sense where she is… but you feel safe and cozy when she is nearby… Perhaps your guardian spirit is sending you a comforting message right now… a word… or a beautiful picture… and in the certainty that you can fly away with your guardian angel at any time, you are now floating in your sphere back to Earth…back to this room… And you are stretching yourself now… and you're here again now, refreshed and awake.

✦ ✦ ✦ ✦ ✦ ✦ ✦ ✦ ✦ ✦ ✦ ✦ ✦ ✦ ✦ ✦

A parent's fears

It's perfectly normal for parents to be afraid for their children. Your daughter should be strapped into the car, cleaning products and other toxic agents must be kept securely stored out of her reach, she must be taught not to touch hot appliances in the kitchen and to stay away from scalding water in the bathtub, swimming pools must be fenced and gated—the issues are endless. And although responsible parents know all this and do their best to safeguard their children against every conceivable accident, still, most children will have accidents at home.

It's important to understand that your daughter may be even more prone to accidents if she is too rigorously protected from experiencing the world around here. For example, she must learn how to fall over in order to learn how to *stop* herself from falling over. I cannot stress enough that falling over is an important and necessary childhood experience!

You will be protecting your daughter more effectively when you show her what can happen, how things work, and why they can sometimes go wrong or hurt her. For example, show your daughter how a door closes and opens. Then demonstrate for her all the places around the door where her little fingers can get caught and injured. Show her how to open and close drawers. Demonstrate (very carefully!) to your child that a lit match and the teapot are hot, that a knife has a sharp edge, and that it's better to slide off a couch and land on your feet than your head. You will be actually protecting your daughter by allowing her to climb trees and roll down hillsides, to balance on one foot, to splash about in a puddle and to walk backwards. Children learn by experience. Being encouraged to gather experience in a protected setting is their best protection against potential dangerous accidents.

✦ ✦ ✦ ✦ ✦ ✦ ✦ ✦ ✦ ✦ ✦ ✦ ✦ ✦ ✦ ✦ ✦ ✦ ✦ ✦

The brave and the not so brave

You will have already noticed that some children are naturally cautious while others are naturally bold. This applies to girls as well as boys. A cautious child should be encouraged to test herself. A daredevil should be permitted to have the experiences they need (and desire) but in a supervised setting.

If your daughter is naturally more daring and extroverted, by all means support her inclinations. Foster her natural talent and curiosity, even if it doesn't precisely fit into the 'feminine' stereotype or doesn't quite match your own ideas about how girls should be. The parent who cultivates and rewards her daughter's strengths with enthusiastic positive reinforcement has an easier time of it than the parent who struggles to eliminate or diminish her weaknesses. Don't be afraid to get caught up in the sheer exhilaration of your daughter's energy! Everything she is allowed to do, she will learn how to do—and everything she learns makes her proud. This pride in herself is the basis for high self-esteem and is the best guarantee that your daughter will become neither a culprit nor a victim. (As a rule, both culprits and victims have low self-esteem. I shall return to this subject later.)

✦ ✦ ✦ ✦ ✦ ✦ ✦ ✦ ✦ ✦ ✦ ✦ ✦ ✦ ✦ ✦ ✦ ✦ ✦ ✦

Fears that are specific to girls

There are some fears that are specific to girls. And from time to time these fears are manifested publicly, such as when a girl is assaulted, raped, murdered or abducted. Crimes against women and girls haunt every parent with a daughter.

How do you feel about this? And how should you handle your feelings? First of all, acknowledge your fear. It doesn't help to suppress it. On the contrary, take a good long look at it. What feeds it? Have you had experiences with (sexual) violence yourself? If you have, it may be advisable for you to try to come to terms with your experiences with the help of professional counselor or therapist. If you don't wish to unconsciously transfer your fears to your daughter, this may be the most effective way break a destructive pattern before it can begin.

If you have had no personal experience of violence, your fears may be based on media coverage (newspaper accounts, radio and television). When a girl dies in an accident or from an illness (as they do daily the world over), it is seldom considered newsworthy. But if she is abducted and murdered, it's news.

Remind yourself that the media's portrayal of life is not balanced and is, in fact, skewed toward the sensational. Nor does the media's portrayal of daily events control our behavior. For example, most of us drive a car whenever we need to, without thinking twice about it, although we know that the chance of having a car accident is far greater than the risk of falling victim to an act of violence.

German bishop and social commentator Dr. Margot Kässmann has commented on this issue: 'On the one hand, it is overtaxing for children to burden them now with the permanent worry of a "pedophile" which, on the other hand, ignores the fact that assault and rape offenders are often relatives, friends or acquaintances. Our fears and precautions are steered in the wrong direction. It is always stressed that self-confidence is the best way of guarding against assault. That is why it's important to strengthen it, rather than spread fear, which diminishes you.'

✦ ✦ ✦ ✦ ✦ ✦ ✦ ✦ ✦ ✦ ✦ ✦ ✦ ✦ ✦ ✦ ✦ ✦ ✦

Take nothing for granted

The possibility of losing your daughter is always present. This should help you see that every day you spend with her is an irreplaceable blessing. There is no better protection than trust and faith! And each smile you share with her is precious. If you knew your daughter would die tomorrow, would you behave differently today?

✦ ✦ ✦ ✦ ✦ ✦ ✦ ✦ ✦ ✦ ✦ ✦ ✦ ✦ ✦ ✦ ✦ ✦ ✦

The problem of 'learned helplessness'

Through psychological testing, it has been established that individual children cope with difficulties in different ways, and that those differences are independent of gender. In one test, with children who were at a similar level of intelligence and education, some responded to a task whose difficulty was steadily increased with renewed effort, while others became confused and, finally, gave up on the task altogether.

Where does this difference in approach and follow-through come from? The children who persisted with the tasks gave themselves a positive pep talk during the course of the test; they were not put off by their mistakes, and predicted a successful outcome for themselves. While the second group of children resigned themselves to failure and declared, 'I can't do this!' the first group persevered, saying, 'I'll try again. Sooner or later, I'll work it out!' It is interesting to note that more girls than boys gave up, although these girls were of above-average intelligence in relation to the group.

Another study points in the same direction. Girls and boys were asked why they achieved a good result on a particular test. While most boys put their good performance down to their own intelligence and industry, many girls said they did well because the tasks were quite easy; that is, they attributed their good performance to favorable external circumstances rather than to their personal strengths and abilities. Further testing shows the reverse is also true: Boys commonly blame failure on external sources, while girls tend to blame themselves.

These results contain important warnings for parents. If your daughter makes a mistake, encourage her to use what she learns from the failure: 'That didn't work, so what does that tell us?' Then, follow up with, 'I'm sure you can do it. There must be another way.'

Thinking can make it so

Learned helplessness is based on the underlying conviction that there is no connection between your personal actions or abilities and the outcome or result. Put simply, it is a belief that 'It doesn't matter what I do—because it won't work anyway!' Does this sentence have a familiar ring to it? If you watch a toddler playing by herself, you'll see her pleasure as she experiments with whatever she discovers around her. She's having fun as she finds a hiding place behind a curtain, makes noise with a pot lid or climbs up onto a chair.

If you interrupt this natural urge to explore and discover and try with comments like, 'Leave it alone,' 'Put it down,' or 'No, that's too hard—you'll never be able to do it!' your daughter may become discouraged and dejected. Soon she may start thinking—believing, 'I won't be able to do this, no matter how hard I try!'

Even as adults, each of us interprets reality in our own way. Do you know the difference between a pessimist and an optimist? A pessimist and an optimist each received a huge pile of horse manure for their birthday. The pessimist is horrified and walks away, saying, 'This sort of shit always happens to me!' The optimist grabs a shovel and starts digging, saying, 'Hurray! With all this shit, it means there must be a pony!'

People who believe in themselves and who don't give up easily assume that everything in life changes: If you can't manage something today, you might be successful tomorrow. Moreover, they look at problems as challenges, situations to be dealt with. And if they fail, they don't automatically blame themselves. Instead, they may try some lateral thinking and look for ways around the obstacle. Such people tend to be creative thinkers, people who are open-minded, and able to embrace the less obvious strategies that might lead to a good outcome. These people know that errors are necessary, and that it is important not to judge a mistake as a negative event without value. Rather, they see a mistake as a spur toward finding a creative solution.

This is why it is so crucial for parents to encourage their daughters. Do not let a day pass without reinforcing your little girl's belief in herself and her capabilities. Use positive statements like, 'You'll get it!' and 'You can do it!' Praise her persistence and foster your daughter's trust in her own competence.

Unfortunately, it is all too common for us to criticize our children and compare them to their siblings or friends. This also takes us in the wrong direction. Comparisons do not motivate; they discourage. Remember, every child is unique with her own set of abilities, knowledge and experiences.

✦ ✦ ✦ ✦ ✦ ✦ ✦ ✦ ✦ ✦ ✦ ✦ ✦ ✦ ✦ ✦ ✦ ✦

Fantasy journeys for adventurous girls (from the age of three)

The following fantasy journeys are only samples. You can create your own simple adventures for your daughter, and include her favorite characters. While you weave the fantasy, your daughter can lie down or sit peacefully, with eyes open or closed.

An animal in the forest

Make yourself quite comfortable...Do you feel the Earth underneath you?... It is carrying you... And now imagine that you're in a beautiful forest... Look around you... perhaps you can hear particular sounds?... Or smell something fragrant?. . . Or feel something soft and furry?... You discover a small, cute animal... Let yourself be surprised by what kind of animal it is... Perhaps you wish to stroke it... Perhaps you want to tell it something...Or does the animal tell you something?... Now it's time to say goodbye to your animal... Now, move your hands and feet and come back into the room, refreshed and awake.

Mountain climbing

Imagine we're climbing a very high mountain... It is stony and steep, but you're very careful about where you place your feet... You know how to do it... We are climbing higher and higher... Above us is the sun... It warms you... Now we're right up on the peak, gazing down into the valley... See how small the houses look from up here? And the cars? And the people?... When we climb back down the slope... we are proud... And so we come back into the room, move our hands and feet and are refreshed and awake.

Dolphins

Today we're going to the beach... It's a warm day, and we're looking out to sea... There, we see a dolphin leap out of the water!... And another one!... Now we feel like swimming... We run into the clear water... Whoosh, how we splash!... We are swimming over to the dolphins... And playing with them... And then we say goodbye to them and swim back to shore... We know we'll meet again another time... And then we return from the beach to this room, move our hands and feet and are refreshed and awake.

Overcoming obstacles (from the age of five)

Today, you are going to ride your favorite horse... Let yourself be surprised by what color he is and what he looks like... He likes you... You can feel that... And now you can get on his back... You are riding the horse...

His mane is flying in your face as you ride to a special place…Have a look around…Feel the special power of this place…Feel your horse's strength, as you ride along a familiar path…Now there's an obstacle in the way, but you know your horse will jump over it easily… Done!. . . Yes, you're a great team. . .And now. . . Another obstacle!…You go for it…You keep riding for a while…Until you're both here again…Say goodbye to your beautiful, gentle horse…Until the next time… And then move your hands and feet and come back into the room, refreshed and awake.

The flying carpet

Just imagine a soft, colorful carpet…It is comfortable to lie down on, but, even better, you know this carpet can fly…Carefully, it takes off…It sails with you out of the window…Down there, your friend is walking through a garden…You wave to her…You fly higher and higher… And you know how to steer the carpet…You know how to make it fly higher and lower and faster and slower… And then you go to special place, someplace where you've wanted to go for a long time…Perhaps it's the zoo…or the home of someone you love who lives far away…or the ocean…or something quite different… And when your journey is finished, you fly back home… Then the carpet comes to rest in your room…And you move your hands and feet, refreshed and awake.

✦ ✦ ✦ ✦ ✦ ✦ ✦ ✦ ✦ ✦ ✦ ✦ ✦ ✦ ✦ ✦ ✦ ✦ ✦ ✦

Girls and pets—a great combination

Many girls (and boys, for that matter) adore animals and would love to have a pet. Learning to be comfortable around animals

and learning to look after them teaches a child about responsibility, compassion and love. Of course I'm not trying to talk you into getting a pet if you don't want one. However, I can assure you, that an animal can enrich your life tremendously, if you are prepared to welcome one into your family.

If your daughter is begging you for a pet, keep in mind that she'll need to be about eight years old before she can be relied on to start looking after an animal on her own. If you acquire a pet when she's younger, be prepared (for the animal's sake) not only to remind her again and again of her care-taking chores, but also to pitch in and help her with them.

✦ ✦ ✦ ✦ ✦ ✦ ✦ ✦ ✦ ✦ ✦ ✦ ✦ ✦ ✦ ✦ ✦ ✦

Pets at school

If you decide against having a pet, or housing regulations restrict you from keeping an animal, perhaps you could ask at your daughter's school about a class pet. At one school I know of, during recess the girls usually race off to their rabbits and guinea pigs while the boys play football. One very positive side effect of the class-room pet trend is significantly lower-than-average aggression among the students! The school where my brother teaches allows plants, mice, fish and more to be kept in classrooms. They are looked after by a team of students, and it is interesting to note that there are more girls on the team than boys.

✦ ✦ ✦ ✦ ✦ ✦ ✦ ✦ ✦ ✦ ✦ ✦ ✦ ✦ ✦ ✦ ✦ ✦

Learning to be responsible for an animal is excellent preparation for taking on parental responsibilities later in life. Observing and caring for animals fosters sensitivity and empathy. Animals also give so much back to their caretakers: They accept us without judgment and their love is unconditional. This experience can be very important and rewarding for children.

Girls and horses—an intimate relationship

From infancy through the kindergarten years, both boys and girls are equally drawn to horses and other animals. But a downright mania for horses begins for many girls immediately before adolescence, around age six to eight. Toy horses (which are available in a staggering variety today) allow girls to connect with horses on a symbolic level, and in their horse games they can express anything and everything that moves them, worries or preoccupies them. Between the ages of six and thirteen, my daughter and her best friend often played for ten hours and longer with toy horses; their games were only interrupted for meals. Sometimes she would slip into the horse's role herself.

Eventually, for many young girls, it's all about *real* horses. Although men still dominate the top-level racing and equestrian

events, in the average stable and riding club there are far more girls and women than boys and men. Why do horses have such a great attraction for girls?

Throughout history, the horse has been man's loyal companion, and carried him safely and swiftly across the world. Apart from the dog, no creature has served humankind with such dedication and versatility, and this remains true to this day. Who would have expected that since the 1950s, when horses finally disappeared from agriculture, that they would still be kept and bred *purely for pleasure* in such large numbers?

The horse is an archetypal symbol, an animal with whom we can communicate in a special way. Riding a horse requires an almost mystical combination of physical and mental communion, intimate contact and trust. Perhaps this makes horses particularly well suited as a paradoxical symbol of power and gentleness, speed and control, beauty and wildness, anxiety and desire. The fact that this very large creature will carry a young girl on its back and let her control it is extraordinarily, almost magically, empowering. And, certainly, girls seem to love to be carried away (in both senses of the phrase) and empowered by horses.

For these reasons (and perhaps others we don't fully understand) girls love horses, and it does them good to associate with them. A girl who learns to ride and care for a horse will gain immeasurably in self-confidence and self-reliance.

What horses can mean to girls

German psychiatrist and author Dörte Stolle writes, 'As a partner in the relationship, the horse is undemanding and free of cares. Girls test out questions like, "What suits me? What do I want to be?" with the horse. And the horse, their horse, conveys that compromises are also feasible without loss of dignity, and adaptability does not mean submission. Qualities that at first look like opposites—greatness, strength and speed versus submission and obedience—can be combined in this powerful companion, which encourages the young rider to try it out herself.'

A girl thus learns that modes of behavior like empathy and gentleness, in combination with their opposites, such as assertiveness and exertion of strength, not only work for the horse, but also for herself when on horseback, and for herself in everyday life. A girl must always assert herself with her horse, while also taking responsibility for its well-being. In addition, riding horses builds a girl's stamina, improves her posture, increases coordination and refines balance.

'The horse seems well suited to convey to girls, in many ways, the pulse that they need for a transition into adult life,' adds Stolle. 'When riding and grooming this symbolic animal, they feel protection and security, but also autonomy and power.'

✦ ✦ ✦ ✦ ✦ ✦ ✦ ✦ ✦ ✦ ✦ ✦ ✦ ✦ ✦ ✦ ✦ ✦ ✦

Learning to ride

Girls as young as five can safely start learning to ride. In time, they will gain such poise and self-assurance that riding and working around horses will become second nature to them. There are therapeutic riding programs that provide hugely enriching and empowering experiences for children with physical and mental disabilities. Even a youngster with a severe handicap can find freedom, acceptance and pleasure on the back of a horse. Horseback riding has also been shown to benefit children with social and behavioral problems.

Owning a horse

If you live in the country, you may consider buying a horse or pony, or you may have ready access to one at a nearby farm or local stable. Keeping a horse or pony can be expensive, so even if you find a bargain, keep in mind that there will also be ongoing costs for hoof care, vet visits, and feed. In many cases, it may be more practical to share your ownership of a horse with another family. However you manage it, if you can arrange for your daughter to have an active interest in horses, you will be giving her one of the most enriching and empowering experiences of her life.

In a nutshell

✦ Self-esteem is the cornerstone of your daughter's emotional development.

✦ High self-esteem helps reduce her fears.

✦ Her self-esteem is likely to be higher when she has a good relationship with her dad.

✦ So-called 'negative' emotions like fear and anger are perfectly normal and should not be suppressed.

✦ We all want to protect our girls from harm, but if they are to learn essential survival skills, we must not be overprotective.

✦ Beware of the trap of 'learned helplessness' by encouraging your daughter to believe in herself and by setting the example of a 'can do' attitude with your own actions.

✦ Pets can play an important role in your daughter's emotional development and her sense of responsibility.

Singing for her supper —Sean

When my daughter, Tessa, was five, our family went for dinner at a bar that permitted children in certain areas. One of these areas had a karaoke competition going on. A stream of men and women, mostly pretty drunk, got up and sang their favorite shower tunes, bowed to the scattered applause, and resumed drinking. Then Tessa decided she wanted a turn. She's always been a great music lover, and her favorite group at the time was the Spice Girls. Her favorite song was 'Stop'. So I got the attention of the karaoke emcee, and a few songs later it was Tessa's turn. I knew she was very nervous, but she strode up to the stage with great determination, took the (huge-looking) microphone in her little hand, and burst into a rendition of 'Stop' in perfect time with the backing track. She forgot the words in only one place in the song, which was great, and through her entire performance she did not move an inch. She stood completely rigid, looking mostly at the opposite wall and occasionally at the familiar faces in the crowd. When she finished, the room shook with applause.

I've never gotten up to sing karaoke in my life, and don't expect I'll start now. I was so proud of Tessa and her courage. She has never shied away from a challenge and has always been keen to try something new. May that never change!

Chapter 5

How Society Conditions Girls

You may already have a good idea about whether the first day of (pre)school is going to be easy or difficult for your daughter. Many children approach this situation with curiosity rather than anxiety, but some find it difficult and need time to adjust. And it's the same for mothers and fathers. Many parents will find it quite easy to see their daughters move into the world, while for others, merely thinking about it makes their hearts heavy.

When your daughter begins her life at an educational institution, whether it is a preschool or day-care center or a primary school, the ideal introduction is for her to get used to both the place and the teacher with a parent present. A more gradual approach will reassure her that she is not being abandoned or given away. The time she spends at school, and what happens to her there, will help to shape who she becomes. Perhaps your daughter will be in a group for the first time, or with boys for the first time. As well as many wonderful experiences, she'll also have to suffer disappointments and overcome conflicts.

Gender stereotyping

Parents can help to ensure that girls and boys are treated fairly and equally in the preschool and the primary school that their daughter attends. Parent-teacher meetings are the appropriate occasions for mothers, fathers and instructors to discuss helping to make the classroom a prejudice-free zone. This is the perfect opportunity to embed new conduct and new areas of experience into the children's routine. Of course, as with everything else, setting the good examples and being the best role models for fair and even-handed treatment is where it all begins.

The use of role-playing in a classroom setting can be a particularly useful exercise for neutralizing gender stereotypes because it prompts the child to take on a role that is opposite to her 'natural' role. (Role-playing is not useful for children under age five, because they're only just discovering their gender identity and they need to actually experience it—often

through exaggerated behavior—before they can safely experiment with it.)

I've had good experiences when I've asked children to create impromptu skits by acting out stories from picture books or well-known fairytales. First I ask them to play their characters according to conventional gender roles. Then I ask them to switch, so that the girls get to slay the dragons and 'rescue' the boys! When role-playing is about fun, everyone can enjoy and learn from it.

For individual activities, there are times when it may be sensible to separate boys and girls and work in single-gender groups, but not because girls are 'better' at one thing and boys are 'better' at another. Research has shown that when the genders comingle, a 'natural' gender-oriented competitiveness tends to take over. Separating the boys from the girls, however, eliminates this. When boys are engaged in woodworking, for example, they can concentrate on honing their skills rather than impressing their female classmates. And if one of the boys hurts himself, he'll have to look to other boys for help and comfort as there are no girls around to look after him or make a fuss. And a girl with innate ability can shine *and* share her talent without the pressure of male competition. Thus, both girls and boys are free to behave and interact without the restrictive expectations of gender stereotypes.

Gender roles and school policy

When you are choosing a school for your daughter (assuming you have more than one option available), read the school's mission statement of educational goals, and look for a policy about gender roles. Talk with the staff and clarify the school's position, and don't be shy about trying to change it if you feel it is inappropriate.

Expressing anger

As we know, little girls often suppress their anger and aggression; they bottle up these feelings rather than expressing them openly and freely. Some girls direct these powerful emotions in on themselves, which can lead to depression and a devalued sense of self-worth. In extreme cases, girls may deliberately hurt themselves, and even kill themselves. Not dealing with or expressing anger and aggression appropriately is unhealthy for all girls of all ages, and indeed for boys as well. The legacy of low self-esteem affects all aspects of a person's life. So while playground altercations between girls and boys may seem relatively insignificant, how a teacher deals with them is extremely important.

Dörte Stolle writes, 'If girls are already supported in pre-school to recognize and take their anger seriously, and are given the opportunity, for example, to test their strength, they will learn that responsibility for others and self-assertion go hand in hand, just as harmony and conflicts do.'

How girls relate

My one-year-old daughter received a toy truck from Santa on her first Christmas and showed not a scrap of interest in it. For most little girls, a conventional boy's toy is uninteresting. Even the colorful Lego® blocks my three sons adored left my daughter cold. She wanted dolls and horses! Linguist Deborah Tannen and many other scientists have demonstrated that most little girls behave differently from little boys, even when encouraged to play with traditionally 'masculine' toys. Social contacts are very important to girls, and even at the age of three, many have a best friend, which in itself is a relatively mature concept.

Whether or not they 'belong' means a great deal to girls. If you tell a story about feelings to a group of three-year-old girls, they will display a clearly defined, social way of thinking insofar as they 'understand' what feelings are. When playing together in a group, girls will usually try to negotiate compromises and be considerate, so as not to upset their girlfriends. Boys at this age, in contrast, often fight each other in order to establish a dominant pecking order.

Deborah Tannen asked pairs of best friends of preschool age, of both genders, to take two chairs into an empty room and occupy themselves. The little girls immediately sat down close to each other and started talking, maintaining eye contact. The boys experimented with putting the chairs in different places; they had very brief verbal exchanges, and hardly looked at each other.

As soon as girls get the concept that someday they'll grow up to become women, they tend to become preoccupied with children, babies and nursing. For little boys, this changes fairly quickly. I remember how my sons, at about two years of age, held their dolls to imaginary breasts. But once they realized they would not actually produce a baby from their bodies, the dolls were tossed into a corner and were not played with again.

I would like to stress, however, that there are always exceptions among children. Not every single girl is interested in dolls. If your daughter would rather play with building blocks, toy cars and stuffed animals, she should be allowed to do so. It is not a good idea to try to influence your daughter to participate in particular games or direct her attention toward a particular toy. On the contrary, watch her play and support her real interests. Give her many opportunities to receive lots of stimulation. If you allow her to follow her joy—that will always be her best motivation.

What About Barbie®?

Barbie has been around—and adored—for more than forty years. Millions of Barbies have been sold in every corner of the world, so chances are pretty good that some day you too will be the parent of a daughter with a Barbie doll. How will you feel about this? Because Barbie looks exactly like a marketing strategist's idea of the average man's dream girl—slender, long-legged, narrow-hipped, with a full bust and long hair—you may wish to consider the influence the she'll have on your daughter.

Author Nicky Marone writes, 'Barbie is more than just a doll. She's the icon of modern femininity, a sacred image of men's fantasy run wild, and [she] undermines many young girls' self-confidence.'

So what are you going to do about Barbie? First, start by looking back at yourself and your childhood. Did you have a Barbie? How did you play with her? Do you remember wanting to look like your Barbie doll? Do you wish you looked like her now?

Nicky Marone writes, 'Part of the problem lies in our own contradictory view of beauty. Most of us, given the possibility, would like to look like Claudia Schiffer or Cindy Crawford. So it's not about not wanting to look like Barbie. We're just resisting the pressure of having to look as beautiful.'

Examine your own ideals of physical beauty before you decide whether or not to buy your daughter a Barbie doll. The pressure on women to look youthful and pretty is so great that most of us concede to this dictate—and of course we pass on this pressure to conform to our daughters.

Shake up the clichés

In the end, buying or not buying a Barbie is okay. If you decide against getting a Barbie for your daughter, be sure to explain why you came to this decision. If you buy her the doll, it's not the end of the world, even though your feminist friends may tell you differently. Either way, explain your position on Barbie to your daughter. Tell her what feelings the doll triggers in you. Make it clear to her that Barbie stand up on her toes because her feet are ready-made for high heels. (Then tell her about all the things that are impossible to do in high heels!)

And don't be surprised if your daughter takes some convincing, because what makes Barbie so irresistible is that she is a

grown woman, not a baby or little girl like so many other dolls. Your young daughter will identify with and want to look like an adult, thus the attraction to Barbie. So what can you do to make Barbie a positive influence on your little girl rather than a negative presence? Join your daughter during some play sessions and make Barbie an airplane pilot or the space shuttle commander, a doctor or veterinarian, a gymnastics star or prima ballerina, make her the leader of an expedition into the jungle or the President of the United States—in short, cast her in leadership roles in which Barbie carries the lion's share of responsibility and/or authority. In this way, at least you can influence your daughter's expectations to a degree. And you may even shake up a few of the current clichés along the way. Nicky Marone offers the following script for a game using Barbie's answering service. I hope it gives you some ideas: 'Hello Barbie, this is Melissa. I have a few questions about the white water rafting trip through the Grand Canyon that you're running this summer. What sort of equipment do I need? Do I need my own helmet and life jacket? What else?' or 'Hello Barbie, don't you remember me? I'm Dr. Carol McIntyre, Professor of Environmental Science at Stanford University. Recently, I learnt from a female colleague that you have just discovered a new type of solar cell. . .'

So, what do you do with Barbie? Make your own decision. I didn't buy one for my daughter, but her grandmother did. And even if she hadn't, I'm sure Barbie would have moved in with us by way of a girlfriend or thanks to birthday or Christmas money. I explained to my daughter why I didn't care for Barbie. In spite of this, my daughter loved playing with her. Then one day, Barbie was out. Soon my daughter had high-heeled shoes of her own!

The truth is, of course, that not everything is under your control. And there's nothing wrong in that, in fact, that's a good thing. But you should always feel free to express your feelings and opinions, so make sure that you do!

✦ ✦ ✦ ✦ ✦ ✦ ✦ ✦ ✦ ✦ ✦ ✦ ✦ ✦ ✦ ✦ ✦ ✦ ✦

Just a little joke . . .

A woman goes into a shop to buy a Barbie doll. The saleswoman shows her the various models: 'This is Equestrian Barbie, which costs $25. Here's Tennis Barbie, which is $22, and that's Wedding Barbie, for $26. And here we've got Divorced Barbie, she costs $100.'

'Why is this last one so expensive?' asks the woman, surprised.

'Because if you take that one, you also get Ken's villa, yacht and private plane.'

✦ ✦ ✦ ✦ ✦ ✦ ✦ ✦ ✦ ✦ ✦ ✦ ✦ ✦ ✦ ✦ ✦ ✦ ✦

Why books are important

Thanks to the popularity (and economic necessity) of day care and preschool, today's children have the opportunity to make friends very early in life. As well as her own family, your daughter may know several other families quite well by the time she goes to elementary school.

But children can also get to know other children and other families through books. Picture books can be browsed in silence, over and over again, whenever your daughter feels like it. And if the book is only text, she will create her own images to go with it, in her mind and perhaps even on paper. Both are creative activities. Watching television is not. Watching television is a completely passive experience. I cannot stress this enough: Television is not a substitute for reading and enjoying books!

Think back to when you were a little girl. Would you like to give your daughter the same experiences you enjoyed as a child? Which were your favorite books? Did you like them for the stories or the illustrations or both? When choosing books for your daughter, consider choosing stories with female heroines in them. But be sure to read them yourself first. Does the image or description of the girl or woman match your ideas about

female role models? Who were the heroines of your childhood? Did they come from books, films or plays? Or did your parents make up stories for you?

Books can influence us throughout our lives. This means that what you read to your daughter and what your daughter reads herself is vitally important. Take your daughter to the library or local bookshop and browse the shelves together; you will make some interesting discoveries about her, about yourself, and about each other.

Fairy tales

Girls and women plays significant roles in virtually every fairy tale that has come down to us through the centuries. This alone is a good reason for you to take them seriously.

Like most things, fairy tales should not be forced on your child. My daughter didn't like them much when she was very young, and only became interested in them as she grew older. Some children don't care for them at all and never grow to love them, while others are utterly enchanted by them. In fact, children who feel drawn to them probably actually need them.

Did you have a favorite fairy tale when you were a child? I had several, and although I've read them probably a hundred times or more, they are still a revelation to me every time. For me, fairy tales are a way to pass along ancient wisdom.

Take *Snow White,* for example. In the original (pre-Disney) version, the mother—not the stepmother—wants to kill her daughter. It's difficult for this woman to see her own beauty fade and watch as her daughter grows more and more lovely. Envy poisons their relationship. Snow White's salvation takes place in the solitude of nature, beyond the seven mountains, while she is with the dwarves, whom she serves. However, they cannot save her from death; that is left to the Prince. He carries her along the bumpy, uneven path in the forest and the poisoned piece of apple falls out of her mouth. Now she is safe. There is a happy ending, as always (even when the story involves excruciating torture or interminably long journeys). Isn't this a comforting message?

In *King Lindwurm,* a German fairy tale, a country is being threatened by a terrifying dragon. It's a shepherd's daughter who saves herself and her homeland. She gives the monster his human form back. She does this by following the advice of a wise old woman. It is not female cunning that does the trick; it is knowledge from a much deeper source.

The heroine in *Sleeping Beauty*, like Snow White, cannot escape her fate; only when the time is right can the male protagonist arrive and kiss her back to life. All the others who tried to reach her stay entangled in the thorns. (But why was the King so stubborn as to permit only twelve of the thirteen wise women to be invited to the feast?)

Fairy tales teach us that nothing is impossible. Through metaphor and allegory, they show us that a path to solution and salvation runs through every impossible task and every dangerous predicament. There is always a moral to every story and it is usually this: if you do not run away from finding a way through, if you do not avoid taking on the task, if you keep an open mind and a willing heart, you will gain access to the wisdom (through a forest, across an ocean, over a mountain) that will lead to your final destination. The message is that by emulating these heroes and heroines, we can all win a kingdom.

Little girls and playing dress-up

My daughter had a strong interest in clothing from an early age. She was able to get dressed and undressed when she was very young, and she derived a lot of pleasure from changing her outfits and trying on clothes. And as soon as she discovered nail polish, she wanted it. It was the same with jewelry. This behavior surprised me, because she didn't get it from me! I don't attach much importance to any of these things and she didn't grow up watching television.

At the age of fourteen, she appeared in front of me one day dressed in a black suit and high-heeled shoes. She was beaming,

and said, 'I'm so looking forward to being able to wear stuff like this every day!'

'Why don't you do it now?' I asked, curiously.

'I don't need to yet,' she said, 'but when I have a professional job, I'll put on something like this every day.'

The many faces of beauty

There is every reason to believe that the desire (among females) to be beautiful is due to social conditioning, and it is a powerful force in the vast majority of cultures and societies. For centuries, women have busied themselves with the manufacture of cosmetics and textiles for clothing. The desire to have a beautifully furnished house and a beautifully clad body—the drive to make an artwork of one's self—is an ancient one.

Nearly every mother takes pleasure in fitting her little daughter with pretty 'feminine' clothes, adorable shoes and even her first jewelry. By contrast, little boys are seldom encouraged to get dressed up. Parents may worry that such behavior might receive ridicule, that their sons will be laughed at and called 'girlie' or gay.

The media's depiction of women

The portrayal of women in magazines, on television, and in film is almost always a distorted version of reality, as we all know. Less beautiful women have only a marginal place in these worlds. Women who do not conform to the 'ideal' are either invisible, or not invited to participate, so we seldom see them, even though they are the majority. And for women who are professionally successful, the more beautiful they are, the more interesting they become— to the media, at least.

Mind you, it has also been proved that beautiful

women don't always have it easy, because others have high expectations of them. From the start, they're expected to be smarter, more affectionate and more pleasant-natured or 'nice'. In addition, many beautiful women believe that they are valued only because of their appearance, and that their achievements are not respected or even considered. These women feel they are rarely taken seriously. Some feel their beauty is a mask they cannot remove and such feelings can lead to self-destruction, through alcohol, drugs or even suicide.

As a little girl, my mother dressed me in dresses and ribbons. During puberty, I lost nearly all interest in these externals, and this has been true for me ever since. Did I want to set myself apart from my older, prettier sister? Perhaps. In families with more than one daughter, each girl takes on a separate role. As soon as the role of 'the pretty one' is taken, the next daughter has to choose another part for herself. She might play 'the intelligent one' or 'the nice one', or 'the rebel' (for more on the importance of birth order, see Chapter 8). Or perhaps I internalized my father's motto: that inner values counted the most. Or perhaps I just chose a different life's work.

✦ ✦ ✦ ✦ ✦ ✦ ✦ ✦ ✦ ✦ ✦ ✦ ✦ ✦ ✦ ✦ ✦

Your daughter and her life's work

After having observed and studied children for more than thirty years, I believe each child has a life's work that she is trying to fulfill. Observe your daughter's interests and notice what gives her pleasure. Because pleasure comes from the heart, it cannot be artificially created by external circumstances. For example, I played intensively with dolls throughout my childhood, and treated them as if they were my children. For me, a life without studying children would have been unimaginable, even if I had not had children of my own.

Once we reach adulthood, many of us accept society's and our family's norms and conditions and expectations. We may do things we really do not want to do because of these external pressures, and in this way we change ourselves, and sometimes turn away from our true life's work. We won't find happiness this way—true happiness comes when you find and fulfill your own personal life's work.

When she is small, your daughter will show you very clearly which way her tendencies and preferences and passions lie—and this applies equally to boys as well.

The word 'education' seems less and less useful to me. In my view, what you should be doing as a parent is better described as 'development', in the literal sense. In other words, watching and supporting your child as she discovers what her life's work is, and helping her develop her abilities. This is what our schools should be doing, but often do not. In order to really find out what your child needs, just observe her, be attentive but not intrusive and offer her a wide variety of experiences. Do not force her in any particular direction.

✦ ✦

In a nutshell

+ Reflect on your own preconceptions about girls in our society.

+ Give some thought to the toys, dolls, etc., that your daughter plays with, and show her there is life beyond Barbie.

+ Girls continue to receive unrealistic and damaging messages about body image from the media.

+ Teach your daughter to not be limited by social conditioning.

+ Books, and especially fairy tales, can be a wonderful source of empowering ideas for girls.

+ Reading, unlike watching TV, spurs the imagination and creative life of a child.

Wishing upon a shooting star —Sean

Just the other evening, I was getting out of the car with my eleven-year-old daughter when she said, 'I want to show you the Southern Cross, Dad.'

'Great,' I replied. 'Let's check it out.'

We walked up the driveway and turned toward the southern sky, and at that very moment a comet went shooting across the darkness right in front of us. I've seen plenty of shooting stars in my time, but this was something special. It sped in a line parallel to the horizon, it shone for a long time, and it was very bright. It was so bright, in fact, it seemed to be so much closer than all the other visible stars.

What was most special about it, though, was that it was the first shooting star that my daughter had ever seen.

'Wow! What a beauty,' I breathed, gazing up in wonder.

'Make a wish!' she cried as she closed her eyes and held her hands up, palms together as if in prayer. (We don't formally pray in our family, and nor does my daughter pray at school, so it was very interesting to see her make this gesture.)

Maybe I should have wished for something beyond the usual 'May everyone in the family have a happy and healthy life', but I didn't. Instead I watched her as she wished for something important. I wanted to ask her what it was, but I knew she wouldn't tell me (because then it won't come true) so I didn't bother. She always says she wants to be a vet when she grows up. Was that what she wished for? I don't know; maybe, maybe not. But if she did, I thought at the time, I am thankful that we live in a world where such wishes can come true. She can be anything she wants to be, and that helps to make me a happy dad.

Chapter 6

Schools and Learning

I n addition to the nurturing experiences you give your daughter at home, you must also be aware of the messages she receives from society at large. Let's now turn to the third significant source and focus of her experience: school.

The news isn't all good

By the time children are in school, girls are often ahead of boys the same age in many areas. They adapt more easily to the school environment, they learn to read and write more quickly, and their social skills are generally more sophisticated. That's what the statistics say. However, these figures may be deceptive.

Girls who don't learn to read and write as quickly as their classmates tend to stand out, and run the risk of being excluded from the group. This is especially devastating for girls because, as a rule, belonging to a group is so important to them.

Although, as we've seen, girls learn differently from boys, this fact is not taken into account, or even acknowledged, by many of our schools. Creating single-gender classes for mathematics, the sciences and technical subjects (that have been traditionally

considered the domain of boys) would be a good place to start. More broadly, school administrators, faculty and curricula designers should (in an ideal world in which time and budgets were limitless) somehow take into consideration the personal family history, experiences and interests of each student.

Choosing the right school

The first thing you can do to help your daughter is, if possible, choose a school that has the best possible conditions for her, and where she is likely to *enjoy* learning. Unfortunately, your child's self-esteem may not be actively recognized and supported in the classroom; it may even be trampled on. This is a very difficult issue to tackle, but it is your duty as a parent to confront the teacher and/or school principal about it.

✦ ✦ ✦ ✦ ✦ ✦ ✦ ✦ ✦ ✦ ✦ ✦ ✦ ✦ ✦ ✦ ✦ ✦

Is this school girl-friendly?

✦ Does the school have policies about Equal Opportunity or Gender Equity that are actually applied and not left to gather dust on a shelf?

✦ Do students know what to do if they're being harassed and bullied? Is there a policy in place about this?

✦ Are there staff members that a girl can approach to discuss personal matters? (They may not necessarily all be women.)

✦ Does the school celebrate International Women's Day? How?

✦ If the school is co-ed, are there any single-gender classes for girls? For which subjects?

✦ Is the curriculum 'gender inclusive'? Or are science, literature, art and history (as examples) taught in a male-centric manner?

✦ Are 'male-dominated' subjects (auto mechanics, woodworking) available to girls? Is cooking and other 'domestic arts' available to boys?

✦ How does the school accommodate girls with disabilities?

✦ Does the school organize girls-only use of particular facilities and spaces, e.g., computers, basketball courts, sports equipment?

✦ Are girls represented equally on student commit-
tees and in school leadership?

✦ Does the school have a uniform? Does it include
trousers, shorts and comfortable shoes for girls
as well as boys?

✦ Does the school encourage young pregnant
women and young mothers to continue their
education?

✦ Are girls allowed to leave class when they are
menstruating? Are sanitary pads or tampons
available in the girls' restrooms? Is there a sanitary pad/tampon disposal unit in every female
toilet cubicle?

✦ ✦ ✦ ✦ ✦ ✦ ✦ ✦ ✦ ✦ ✦ ✦ ✦ ✦ ✦ ✦ ✦ ✦

Your daughter may be described as 'reserved in class', or 'not
living up to her potential'. But what do these tags actually mean?
Isn't there room for all types of children? If your daughter has

academic challenges, it is especially
important that you support her
and show her that you love her
despite these difficulties. Meet with
her teachers and arrange for extra
tutoring or supervised study. And
be sure to pay attention to your
daughter's extracurricular interests
as these may indicate her academic
strengths and weaknesses.

✦ ✦

The Helene Lange School

The Helene Lange School in Wiesbaden, Germany, is a high school in which each class is led by two class teachers, one male and one female. Conventional curricula have been largely abandoned in favor of practical, hands-on, community-oriented projects. As examples, the school sends students to 'work' in an elder-care hostel, a kindergarten and a hospital. Classes are kept small, ensuring that each student receives individual attention. Personal responsibility, accountability and cooperation are qualities that are prized and emphasized. The school's theatre program is well-known and highly regarded all over the country. The teachers describe themselves as 'trainers' rather than 'lecturers', and regularly attend continuing education courses to improve their skills.

✦ ✦

Girls and math and science

As a rule, girls tend not to do as well as boys in standardized math tests. There are various theories about why this is so. One theory promotes a hormonally based difference between male and female brains as the reason; another theory suggests that the differences between the way girls and boys are treated at home and at school can account for differences in scholastic performance, specifically in math and science.

In 1995 and 1996, *The Third International Mathematics and Science Study* was conducted in which half a million pupils in the fourth, eighth and twelfth grades in twenty-one countries were assessed. In math and the sciences, boys in all the countries except South Africa achieved higher results than girls, and the older they were, the greater the difference. Although the respective differences within the girls' group and within the boys' group were greater than the differences between the genders, the test results did seem to prove that boys test better than girls in these study areas.

If one examines the results more closely, however, as author Susan Gilbert did, it is clear that these differences only applied to white students. Moreover, she established that non-white girls did better than non-white boys in arithmetic. Thus, the decisive factor seems to be that many (white) parents believe that girls are less talented at math than boys. And more importantly, it seems that their daughters think the same thing!

By the beginning of puberty, girls seem to lose interest in math, which puts them at a disadvantage, because math is the basis for so many areas of study. But should girls really study math? Does it pay off for us? Evidently not always, according to Susan Gilbert. For together with their dislike of mathematical subjects, she claims that some girls accept the prejudices of their contemporaries: 'A girl who is good at math is unattractive to boys.' I don't believe things are so simple. When I asked my fifteen-year-old daughter about this, she smiled and said she thought most boys would prefer an intelligent girlfriend. But even in her class, the math geniuses are all boys.

Learned helplessness

Why is it that girls sometimes just seem to give up and give in to gender stereotypes? Instead of viewing a mistake as a challenge and something they can use as a basis for improvement, they shrug and say, 'I'm a girl. I don't have to be good at that.'

In a study by Michigan University in the 1980s, thousands of children were tested to identify the roots of the gender difference in achievement in math. The study questioned children *and* their parents. During the early primary school years, parents assessed the mathematical skills of their sons and daughters as relatively equal; however, by the time their children reached the end of primary school, most parents believed there were distinct differences. The parents who assumed math was particularly difficult for girls actually underestimated their daughters' performance. If a girl struggled with her math homework, most parents sympathized rather than encouraged her. And when she received a good math grade, she was praised less for her mathematical skill and more for her hard work. Not surprisingly, doubts about natural mathematical skill among girls also came from the girls themselves!

Encouraging persistence

It is clear that if you treat girls differently when it comes to math, and expect less from them, they are more likely to get poorer results. This is how a self-fulfilling prophecy works. This means that it is important for you to encourage your daughter in *all* her schoolwork, and indeed in all other areas of endeavor. Girls can achieve good results in math, just as boys can. *The issue is what is expected of them, and thus what they expect of themselves.* This observation echoes what we noted earlier when parents react to a daughter's mistake or failure at a task (see pages 78–81). You need to encourage and reward persistence. This support shows that you believe your daughter can and will succeed, and these are the kinds of positive reinforcement that builds her self-esteem.

✦ ✦ ✦ ✦ ✦ ✦ ✦ ✦ ✦ ✦ ✦ ✦ ✦ ✦ ✦ ✦ ✦ ✦ ✦

A learning difference

American psychologist David C. Geary investigated how girls and boys go about solving problems. He revealed that boys will tend to see an exercise pictorially, or as an image or series of images, whereas girls respond to verbal instruction, that is material presented in spoken or written form. He recommended that teachers and parents of boys represent verbally formulated tasks graphically, and parents and teachers of girls should consider a verbal approach to problems.

✦ ✦ ✦ ✦ ✦ ✦ ✦ ✦ ✦ ✦ ✦ ✦ ✦ ✦ ✦ ✦ ✦ ✦ ✦

Styles of learning

In my opinion (and experience), if math is taught using limited materials that don't suit a girl's preferred style of learning, she will probably fail at it. A friend of mine once showed me the arithmetic materials used in Montessori schools. It is clear and simple, and extremely appealing to the eye. I am sure that if I had been taught with such materials, I would have enjoyed and understood math, too.

However, the girls are closing the gap! The gap in test results is narrowing, and fewer people now believe the old ideas about girls being 'naturally inferior' at math. Studies also show that girls get better grades overall than boys.

However, in comparison to men, there are still relatively few women taking on the male-dominated math-oriented professions, regardless of how well they did in math at school. Why is this?

One explanation suggests that what a girl perceives as society's expectations affect her choice of occupation. Even today, a girl may feel pressured by her family or her peers to pursue a more typically 'female' career.

Not all women want to reach the top

It is common knowledge that fewer women reach top management positions, even in traditional 'women's professions.' When I recently discussed this with a social scientist, she said, 'Yes, but we women don't want those positions.' She was single and living alone and had declined several management positions because she didn't want the responsibility associated with them. Perhaps women have less desire for power. On the other hand, there are also many women struggling in what still feels like a 'man's world'. Although the highest positions should be available to all, the 'glass ceiling' seems to appear overhead sooner or later. Once a woman reaches it, she will either shatter it or progress no further and, if the latter, without knowing why.

How to encourage your daughter

You have many opportunities to encourage and support your daughter so that she will be successful in school and ultimately choose an occupation that matches her preferences and abilities. The following ideas might be helpful:

✦ Promote your daughter's spatial-visual imagination. Spatial-visual skills develop through practice and experience with suitable toys. Let your daughter play with wooden building blocks and Legos®. Sports activities are also helpful.

✦ Encourage your daughter not to give up, but to keep working toward a solution. If she's having trouble with a particular task, try saying, 'Maybe you haven't found the right method yet. Let's try it together.' Or 'If you don't solve it now, put it down, and have a look at it later. Often you gain a fresh perspective when you come back to something after a break.'

And when it comes to math:

✦ Have a look at the Montessori math materials and use them if you think they would help your daughter be more confident and capable with math.

✦ Encourage your daughter's math talents by using mathematical questions in your everyday conversation, 'There are five of us in the family. But Tom is at his friend's house, and Dad won't be home until late. How many places will we set at the table?' When you cook, ingredients may have to be doubled or halved. Involve your daughter as you revise the recipe.

✦ As a father, involve your daughter in what are typically 'men's' jobs.

✦ Encourage your daughter to take part in or visit you when you're on the job. This may not always be possible, of course, but it may be more possible than you think if you apply a little creativity.

✦ Teach your daughter how to handle money and involve her in everyday money transactions.

✦ Involve your daughter in any furnishing or home renovation tasks you are undertaking. There are calculations and measurements to be made and she can help with them.

✦ Give her a chance to have fun with math and science. Microscopes and telescopes may be more fun than Barbie!

Positive learning

Make yourself comfortable and watch your breathing, how it comes and goes, all by itself... And then imagine that you are strolling through a lovely, cool forest... You look around and notice a particularly beautiful tree... You want to pause here ... It is such a beautiful and peaceful place... All at once, you feel the presence of a kind fairy... She is a wise, loving, wonderful woman, who comes from a place where everything is possible... She wishes to teach you something, something that you want to learn . . . And now she is showing you what it is . . . And you've got all the time in the world, all the time you need, to watch closely or to listen to her . . . (long pause) . . . And now you say thank you and goodbye, in the certainty that you may return to this place at any time . . . Whenever the fairy wants to teach you some-thing, you can return to this special tree . . . And when you've made sure that you remember everything along the path, you go back through the forest . . . And you come back here again, move your hands and feet, and you are completely returned, refreshed and awake.

In a nutshell

✦ Investigate 'girl-friendly' schools before you make a choice for your daughter.

✦ Underachievement in math among girls is primarily due to parental attitudes, inappropriate teaching materials and gender stereotyping in schools.

✦ *Your* attitudes about your daughter's scholastic abilities will dramatically influence your daugh-ter's attitudes about her abilities.

Helping them achieve their (individual) dreams —Jeanette

I have two daughters, twenty-three months apart in age. They have similar talents in sports and artistic endeavors but, at the same time, very different abilities and goals. Elysia, my eldest, from the day she could walk at the age of nine months, would climb everything in sight. This included a set of sturdy book-cases in the living room, which we kept empty so she could do this without danger of hurting herself. Subsequently, she never fell or tired of doing this.

As she grew up, she showed some talent in certain sports, and always felt confident in her general athletic ability. At the end of each school year she was nominated for 'Sports Girl of the Year' and would be narrowly beaten in a very competitive field. Finally, after ten years, she was nominated as 'Sports Girl for 2003' for the whole school, and she won. This was not only a very proud moment for her parents, who had enjoyed all of her sporting successes over the years, but also for Elysia herself. She has now given up most of her sporting interests, except weekend soccer, now that she is in senior high school with its many social and academic demands. Ultimately, the confidence she developed as a result of her sporting activities will serve her well when she is an adult.

As for my other daughter, Allegra also enjoys soccer but has an interest in drama and now attends a Performing Arts High

(continued)

School. Her talent for self-expression was nurtured and encouraged by wonderfully creative teachers at her primary school. Even in those early years, she was very clear in her mind that she wanted to perform. So, like all good parents, we helped her develop her talent. She never showed any fear or nervousness when performing and it was wonderful when she achieved her goal and was accepted into a Performing Arts High School. This highly creative environment, however, can be quite competitive and even somewhat intimidating with such a large pool of talent.

Allegra began to feel nervous and insecure about performing in front of her peers and started to miss out on certain opportunities the school provided. What did we do? We enrolled her in intensive drama classes to build her confidence back up and gradually put her in competitive situations to help reduce her anxiety. Is it succeeding? Yes. Bit by bit, Allegra's confidence is returning, and hopefully will return to what it was in primary school.

Chapter 7

Becoming a Young Woman

Puberty and the associated developmental steps present significant challenges for all children and their parents. While nine- to ten-year-old girls are often confident and self-assured, by the time they are thirteen, fourteen or fifteen they often become confused, agitated and insecure. This usually has less to do with parenting style and more to do with hormonal changes combined with the new role expectations each girl faces as she approaches adolescence and adulthood. Furthermore, your daughter probably won't automatically come to you for help with these challenges. At this age, her girlfriends will become extremely important to her. Also, she may turn to her favorite teachers or other trusted adults for guidance, and they may be more suitable mentors at this stage in her life.

The journey from puberty through emerging adulthood is a critical one. It will prepare her for an independent life away from home and you. Leaving home and family is one of the most important steps in every person's life, and doing it with love on both sides is crucial. If this separation is less than successful, there can be a lifelong and unhealthy dependency ('mamma's boys' or 'daddy's girls'). These young people have difficulty detaching

from their parents and continue to need parental support in a variety of ways throughout their lives.

What does puberty mean?

But let's return to puberty: What does it mean and what happens during this stage in a girl's life?

The word 'puberty' comes from the Latin *pubertas,* meaning sexual maturity. In fact, the root of the word is related to the Latin *pubes,* meaning pubic hair. However, before this starts to appear on your daughter's body, there must be an increase in the production of the sex hormone estrogen. This may happen as early as age eight or nine. How does her body know that it is ready for puberty? Why do some girls reach puberty sooner than others? Body weight plays a significant role in this. At about 80 to 90 pounds, the hormonal control system signals that it's time to begin the move into womanhood.

Hormones act in a similar way to yeast or baking powder. They stimulate physical growth and help to trigger certain behaviors. Nursing a baby, for example, is made possible by the action of the hormone prolactin, which causes the breasts to produce milk. Steroid hormones help to stimulate brain growth during puberty by actually boosting the mechanisms for thinking and questioning. Estrogen activates your daughter's body to grow, to fill out and become rounded, to feel adult sexual pleasure and desire and to seek sexual satisfaction.

The search for personal identity

In the search for personal identity, both girls and boys will ask themselves important questions:

✦ Who am I?

✦ How do others see me?

✦ What will I do with my life!?

During this process, our daughters will come up against the barriers of culturally defined femininity time after time. They will be asked to consider the expectations of their family and society, and, where possible, to fulfill them. 'With characteristics like pleasantness, adaptability, restraint, they conform to social expectations,' writes Dörte Stolle.

The pressures during puberty

It is during adolescence that your previously self-confident daughter may begin to doubt her abilities and question herself in many different contexts. Images of female beauty that she sees in the media shows her how an 'attractive' woman *has* to look, and, of course, how important it is to be attractive. She will begin to see that it's hard to be 'a good girl' and at the same time withstand the pressures of performance and competition. This makes it difficult for an insecure girl to be accepting of and satisfied with her body. When I asked my daughter what makes girls so insecure, the first item on her list was magazines that are aimed specifically at women and teenagers. 'The magazines tell you how to apply make-up, how to do your hair, and how to dress. And if you don't look as good as the models, you're disappointed,' she explains. Eighteen-year-old Elke writes, 'Sometimes I want to be like the female Pope in the Middle Ages, who was a very courageous woman. But usually I think first about what others want of me, particularly boys and men. For them I know I must be sexy yet modest, flirtatious but devoted, soft and adaptable but independent and not too needy, slim as well as curvy; I must have a pouting mouth, beautiful hands, pretty hair, not too many muscles. That's how they like us to be, I think. Because I know this, I play on it occasionally, I use it.'

Adolescence is the cornerstone, the hub of a girl's psychic, social and biological development. On the one hand, she will experience traditional role allocation, but at the same time she will also see unconventional, flexible lifestyles. She will see young actresses and pop stars earning millions, while her own parents may struggle financially despite working long hours for a lifetime. Finding your way in this jungle of possibilities isn't easy.

✦ ✦ ✦ ✦ ✦ ✦ ✦ ✦ ✦ ✦ ✦ ✦ ✦ ✦ ✦ ✦ ✦ ✦ ✦

Mentors

For many young women, having a mentor—an experienced adult who can share her life experience—is a great help. A mentor can be a teacher, instructor or coach (perhaps a horse-back riding instructor, gymnastics coach, or ballet teacher), a trusted neighbor or family friend, or a non-immediate family member such as a grandmother, a favorite aunt or godparent. A mentor may sometimes function as a mediator during disagreements among immediate family members.

✦ ✦ ✦ ✦ ✦ ✦ ✦ ✦ ✦ ✦ ✦ ✦ ✦ ✦ ✦ ✦ ✦ ✦ ✦

The role of the peer group

During adolescence, being a member of a group of girls around the same age is very important. Peer groups at school or in the community give girls a sense of identity that is independent of their families, provide a forum for the exchange of ideas and information and provide a support network, or a feeling of 'us versus the world.' Within the context of a group, a girl can safely experiment with haircuts, clothing and make-up. Time spent together and on the phone helps girls develop an individual and group identity and the opportunity to practice interpersonal social skills.

Intense friendships are common at this stage, and serve many positive purposes. Girls learn to cope with individual weaknesses, they learn to say no and to become empathetic conversation partners. Close teenage friendships offer girls the chance to experience respect and recognition. Peer groups can also take on mentoring functions, as experiences are shared. During this life stage it is often easier to learn from a contemporary than from an adult.

It is a struggle for some girls to develop a healthy and positive identity these days, especially if their looks don't match the current images of beauty and desirability projected by the all-pervasive media. Our daughters are under pressure in ways we were not, and it may be all but impossible for them to avoid conforming to stereotypes, at least for a period of time. Your daughter needs your understanding and patience at this time in her life. Above all, listen to her. (And don't take her moods to heart!)

The female cycle

When a girl enters the female cycle, this is much more than simply beginning to menstruate. There are four phases of this cycle, which I like to compare with the seasons.

The first phase starts with the maturation of the egg in the follicle, which is a cell nucleus in the ovary. So that the egg can mature, the body produces the hormone estrogen, which also activates the womb and breasts. This phase nicely corresponds to early spring: at the Earth's core, everything is already growing, even if outside it still appears to be winter and nature seems to be sleeping. Within your daughter's body, the possibilities are just beginning to emerge.

In the second phase, there is ovulation. Between about the fourteenth and the sixteenth day of the cycle, a mature egg moves into the incubating sleeve. This phase corresponds to late spring when trees begin to blossom, attracting insects with their colors and fragrances, thus assuring fertilization. I think of this phase as the fruitful period of the female cycle; many women feel particular pleasure in their sexuality during this phase.

In the third phase, the egg is changed into the so-called gestagen nucleus. This generates gestagen, which is made up mostly of progesterone, a hormone that induces the womb to prepare to receive the egg. The womb's lining thickens and is enriched with nutrients. This phase corresponds to summer when the fruit is ripening, and unfertilized flowers start to wither. There are no special hormones needed now. The egg has matured. Estrogen and progesterone fall to their lowest levels. During this phase, your daughter may feel bad-tempered and aggressive or even depressed. In the body, the gestagen cells and womb lining now begin to decompose.

The womb lining detaches itself in the fourth phase, which we call menstruation. This phase corresponds to autumn. What kind of 'blood' is it that flows out of the body? Explain to your daughter that it contains vitamins, proteins, iron, copper, magnesium, kalium, calcium and other mineral salts (nutrients that some people spend a small fortune on in the form of supplements), as well as a large number of immune cells.

When you understand the complete cycle, you can handle your daughter's mood fluctuations with more consideration. No female remains unaffected by the changes the cycle brings!

First menstruation

When I had my first period, I was eleven years old and all alone. My mother was seriously ill and nobody had prepared me for menstruation. There were no sanitary napkins, so I had to work out on my own how I could best manage my bloodied underpants. Many girls of my generation had similarly embarrassing and even frightening experiences. Previous generations of American girls referred to menstruation as 'the curse' or 'being on the rag'. Older European women often referred to menstruation as 'your filth' or 'your shit', or simply refused to talk about it altogether.

Fortunately, the mothers of my generation have made sure not to repeat this humiliating behavior. When their daughters were quite young, they showed them that they bled once a month and explained that this special event belongs to all women. It is important for your daughter to know that menstruation is connected to the ability to bear children. Once she appreciates this, she can feel proud when she experiences her first period, and make no secret of it. For her, it will be a reason to celebrate.

I suggest that you talk with your daughter before she is likely to have her first period. Ask her what she would like to do when it happens. Would she like to celebrate it in some way? Author Margaret Minker offers a suggestion: 'Do you want to have a red feast? Then everyone comes in red clothing, you eat red food and celebrate your life. Older and younger women could write down why it is beautiful being a woman and you could sing and dance together.'

Most girls I know today would think the idea of such a party hugely embarrassing, but I still think it's a good idea to suggest something like it. This way, your daughter will at least know that you don't think she has anything to feel ashamed of. Perhaps she would like to just go out somewhere nice to eat. Perhaps she would like to receive a symbolic gift, perhaps a ring or a special pendant to signal her transition to womanhood.

✦ ✦ ✦ ✦ ✦ ✦ ✦ ✦ ✦ ✦ ✦ ✦ ✦ ✦ ✦ ✦ ✦ ✦ ✦ ✦

Help with menstrual pain

Many girls today reach for pain-relief tablets for their periods without hesitation, because their mothers encourage them to do so. I would caution mothers and daughters about this as it can lead to dependence on medication. As an alternative to pharmaceuticals, why not consider safe and natural herbal remedies that have been tested over centuries? Lady's mantle (of the genus *Alchemilla*) and yarrow (of the genus *Achillea*) have been shown to provide effective treatment. If you are lucky enough to have a garden, or even a small balcony, you can grow your own herbs and either prepare your remedies yourself or teach your daughter how to make her own preparations. Knowing that she can help herself will boost her self-confidence and give her a sense of control over her life. Natural food stores, herb shops, many pharmacies and mail-order venues are also reliable resources for herbal remedies. If you find home treatments less effective, consult a physician about managing your daughter's symptoms.

✦ ✦ ✦ ✦ ✦ ✦ ✦ ✦ ✦ ✦ ✦ ✦ ✦ ✦ ✦ ✦ ✦ ✦ ✦ ✦

Massaging the belly can also be helpful and relaxing. Purchase or prepare a massage oil with jojoba or almond oil, and add the following:

✦ 1 drop of essential rose oil

✦ 1 drop of Roman chamomile oil

✦ 1 drop of cypress oil

✦ 2 drops of marjoram oil

Another technique is to use visualization exercises to help soothe menstrual pain and cramping.

✦ ✦

Soothing menstrual pain

Make yourself comfortable with a blanket and hot water bottle…Close your eyes, and get used to the welcome darkness…Imagine that it is helping you to forget your everyday cares…Feel the security that the darkness is giving you … and imagine that the darkness contains everything…Look at the night sky…How dark it is…Look at the stars and galaxies, the Milky Way…Look at the moon and its glimmer…Envelop the darkness in your body as a source of renewal and transformation…As each night allows the new day to appear…The darkness is the source of all being…We are returning from the darkness and coming back to ourselves…Enjoy the darkness for a little while longer…And then come back here into the room…Move your hands and feet and come completely back, refreshed and awake.

✦ ✦

✦ ✦ ✦ ✦ ✦ ✦ ✦ ✦ ✦ ✦ ✦ ✦ ✦ ✦ ✦ ✦ ✦ ✦ ✦

Teenage pregnancy in Australia
by Steve Biddulph

What are the facts?

First, the good news: the number of teenagers giving birth has plunged in the last twenty years. Nationally the rate peaked in 1971, when 5.5 percent of all teens got pregnant, and today it is less than 2 percent, a reduction by almost two-thirds. We are doing well internationally, too: teen pregnancy in Australia is less than half that of the United States and only two-thirds the rate of New Zealand or Great Britain.

But teenage pregnancy is still a concern if you live in an economically depressed or more remote region. In very remote parts of Australia, the teenage birth rate is 9 percent, compared with 4.4 percent in suburban areas and only 1 percent in major cities. It even makes a difference which state you live in: the Northern Territory has six times the rate of Victoria. Tasmania, Queensland and Western Australia all have twice the rate of Victoria and the Australian Capital Territory. New South Wales and South Australia are about halfway between.

Why is this?

The drop in teen pregnancy appears to be due to better education, contraception use, and availability of abortion. However, there is still plenty of room for improvement. For instance, the abortion rate among teenagers is the same as the rate for live births. Between 2 and 3 percent of teenage girls have abortions before the age of twenty. Whatever your views on abortion, this is far from an ideal situation. On the other hand, 95 percent of teenagers are managing to avoid unwanted pregnancies, which is pretty good.

What prevents teenage pregnancy?

Let's be clear that teenage pregnancy is neither bad nor wrong. In fact, it's been the median age for human motherhood throughout most of our history. It's just that in today's society, it's a struggle for a young couple, or a young woman on her own, to avoid poverty unless they are able to finish their education, get some qualifications, and manage the cost and time demands that a baby requires. (There have been some successful back-to-school programs for teen moms in high schools, which aim to help young mothers learn parenting skills as well as encourage them to finish their education. And remarkably, these programs have been found to *reduce* the pregnancy rates in those schools, in other words, it's good for other students to see the reality of teen parenting firsthand.

So what can you do to help your daughter avoid getting pregnant too young? It turns out that the way you live *your* life as a parent is the greatest contributing factor in your daughter's decisions regarding pregnancy and motherhood.

According to a study by Julie Quinlivan, Professor of Obstetrics at Melbourne University and head of the Royal Women's Hospital's 'Young Mums' clinic, about a third of teenage mothers actually plan their pregnancies, and believe that having a baby will be one of the most positive experiences of their lives.

Professor Quinlivan told the *Sydney Morning Herald* that the appeal of getting pregnant, for some girls, is the chance to build a loving family life for themselves, which is often in contrast to their own experience. She found that teen mothers were much more likely to have come from fractured families, and sought love and security through the birth of a baby. Unfortunately, this motivation can be a recipe for disaster without a lot of support.

Quinlivan found that more than half of the teen moms she studied had been five years old or younger when their parents had separated (which is five times higher than the national average rate). They were also ten times more likely to have been exposed to parental violence. For some girls, creating a family was a way to escape. According to Quinlivan, 'If you have an adverse early life, you want to grow up fast, and get out early to feel safer.'

One of the strongest themes to emerge from interviews with pregnant teenagers was their idealization of motherhood. More than half expected it would be the most exciting event of their lives (although that's true for most of the rest of us, too!). The problem lies in what makes it exciting, that is, the prospect of a baby's unconditional love. Quinlivan found, 'This comes through all the time, that "this is someone who loves me." '

Her research showed that reducing teen pregnancy was not simply a matter of improving sex education or access to contraception. Rather, it was one of 'breaking the cycle', as the children of teenage parents were more likely to become teenage parents themselves. About two-thirds of the young mothers Quinlivan studied are doing well. 'The ones who do the best have family support, go back to school, and don't have another baby straight away.' But nearly half of teenage mothers have another child within two years of their first, which makes it difficult for them to continue their education.

So, to conclude, if you don't want your teenage daughter to become a mother:

✦ Make sure you and your partner are good role models, as individuals and as a couple, for her.

✦ Don't talk about respect, *demonstrate* what a respectful relationship is to her.

✦ Give her unconditional love.

✦ Stay involved in her life.

If you are living in a violent marriage, what should you do? Do you leave and become another divorce statistic? Or should you stay and become a role model for violent relationships? Perhaps the only 'right' answer is to, first, get help. Because every step you manage to take toward safety, security and continued involvement with your family will strengthen the safety net around your daughter.

And what if your young daughter does become pregnant? First and foremost, your support and understanding of her emotional and physical health is paramount. If she decides to go through with her pregnancy, your encouragement for her to continue her schooling, and your acceptance of her new baby (and hopefully her partner) will be essential for a successful family outcome.

✦ ✦ ✦ ✦ ✦ ✦ ✦ ✦ ✦ ✦ ✦ ✦ ✦ ✦ ✦ ✦ ✦ ✦ ✦ ✦

Staying connected

As long as you stay connected with your daughter during adolescence, you won't lose her. This is both ancient wisdom and modern common sense, and you'll see it confirmed, again and again, throughout your relationship with your daughter. The quality of your conversations, meaning the quality of your *communication,* with her will decide the quality of your relationship with her. I would like to suggest some ground rules that may improve or enhance your communication with your teenage daughter.

✦ When you talk about your feelings, your observations, your ideas, try to use 'I' sentences, rather than resorting to judgmental 'you' sentences. For example, 'I'm upset by the mess in this room because I can't find the CD I was looking for,' instead of 'No one can find anything in this room because you're such a slob!' or 'I loved the way you looked in that black skirt last Friday. I think it made your waist look tiny,' rather than 'You look

ridiculous in that dress! You're not leaving the house looking like that!' Express yourself by owning your feelings rather than turning them into an accusation your daughter can't refute.

✦ Avoid generalizations, like 'You're *always* late' or 'You've *never* washed those jeans, have you?' or 'Why does *everything* end up on the floor in your room?' Reproaches that are expressed in this way, even if they are valid at the time, are *dis*couraging rather than *en*couraging to your daughter. How can she ever live up to your expectations if she 'always' does 'everything' wrong and 'never' does anything right? When you speak in generalizations and absolutes, you don't allow for any potentially positive exceptions. Instead, try to talk about specific things and encourage the behavior or values you'd like to see. Instead of, 'You forgot to set the table *again,'* try 'That was so great that you set the table last night without my even having to ask. Could you help me out and set it again tonight?' And rather than, 'What did you hate about the movie, or was it just because it was the one I wanted to see?' try 'There were some things I really liked about the movie and a few things that were disappointing. How about you?'

✦ Always try to deal with specific, real-time situations rather than vague generalities. Instead of 'You watch way too much television,' try 'No, it's not all right for you to turn on the TV now. We agreed you'd do your homework first.' And rather than 'Why do I have to remind you to walk the dog every single day?' try 'The dog hasn't been walked yet. Please take him out so we can get you to cheerleading practice on time.'

✦ *Always* take her feelings seriously and express what you notice about them: 'I can see that you're upset. What happened at school today?' or 'You seem unhappy about something. Even if it's something private, you know we can talk about it.' Or 'Obviously, you're bored right now. If you're interested another time, I'd suggest…'

✦ Every person has the right to their own feelings, and your daughter has the right to express hers, just as you have a right to express yours. When your daughter shares her feelings, you may want to take this expression as a request for something to be discussed later. Passionate feelings require a cooling-off period before their causes can be talked about calmly.

✦ Pay your daughter compliments frequently, but be genuine. Empty praise is just that—empty. In families where everyone feels acknowledged and appreciated, the ratio is (generally) one critical comment for every five positive ones. How does your family rate in comparison?

There are so many ways to say things and so many ways to give positive reinforcement *along with* a critical evaluation. More often than not, however, we tend to forget that a critique isn't just about criticism. And because we've heard critical comments all our lives from our own parents, teachers, colleagues and others, we tend to use them ourselves. Be sure to check your vocabulary for the following conversation and self-esteem killers and try to avoid the following:

- ✦ What is the matter with you?

- ✦ How many times do I have to tell you?

- ✦ Can't you be more like your sister?

- ✦ What are you crying about now?

- ✦ Typical girl!

- ✦ Let me do it.

- ✦ If you do that, you'll be…

- ✦ Just look at the mess you've made.

- ✦ What on Earth do you have on?

- ✦ How will you ever…?

- ✦ How many times are you going to make this same mistake?

Loosening the leash

Young people know that family is very important. It shapes them, gives them security, and is the place where they can deal with conflicts and build a foundation for life. But adolescence can be a testing time for everyone.

Suddenly, your daughter will insist on being allowed to: go to parties, movies and dance clubs, smoke cigarettes, drink alcohol, wear make-up and revealing clothing, go on dates with boys, travel around the country or around the world with friends her age. Out of the blue, you'll be badgered with the question, 'Mom, can I...? Dad, can I...?' If you say 'yes,' you'll probably die of anxiety. If you say 'no,' a volcano erupts.

How much freedom?

Some parents insist on keeping their children on a relatively short leash. Sports and organized extracurricular activities offer some outlets for personal freedom, but usually within a structured and supervised environment. Their daughters tend to live at home longer and often conform more closely to their parents' expectations. But if the parenting style is too restrictive, teenage girls will often react with stubborn resistance or frustratingly evasive behavior.

The family that gives a child a reasonable and age-appropriate amount of freedom gives her room to breathe and space to grow into who she wants to be. Girls raised this way tend to value good communication, have less trouble separating from their parents and can analyze social conventions with a critical eye. But it's unwise to loosen the leash too much, as excessive freedom can be just as dangerous as repressive control, as we will see later in the chapter.

✦ ✦ ✦ ✦ ✦ ✦ ✦ ✦ ✦ ✦ ✦ ✦ ✦ ✦ ✦ ✦ ✦ ✦

Handing over responsibility

The challenge for you as a parent is to be present and communicative with your children, and at the same time to gradually hand over responsibility to them as they grow up. This will help make their separation from you as smooth as possible.

✦ ✦ ✦ ✦ ✦ ✦ ✦ ✦ ✦ ✦ ✦ ✦ ✦ ✦ ✦ ✦ ✦ ✦

Once your daughter reaches puberty, you cannot expect to raise her the way you did when she was small. It's less about pro-

tecting and empowering her and more about walking beside her and constantly staying in dialogue with her. Once in a while, you may be able to set up an occasion for an important conversation. But more often than not you won't be able to do this. You'll just have to wait attentively for the right moment to bring up certain issues with her. Usually, the deepest and most meaningful talks just happen spontaneously. And if you don't take advantage of these precious opportunities when they arise, you'll waste most of your chances. Never use the excuse 'Not right now, honey, I'm too busy, but maybe we can talk about it later.'"

I cannot specifically advise you about what you should and should not allow your daughter to do. As parents, you must decide these perimeters and accept responsibility for them for yourselves. However, it is vital that you know what your positions are on the big issues and be able to justify them. Your daughter needs your support and your perspective. However, whether she does what you recommend or not is another matter. Don't be surprised if she occasionally contradicts you. This is completely normal. She must learn to find her own way and test herself, and arguing with you is one way she will learn to do that.

'Puberty is a period of unbelievably big egotism, narcissism and uncertainty,' writes Margot Kässmann. 'It seems to me that young people are so preoccupied with themselves that they don't really manage to notice others deeply. I suppose parents have to expect that the seed they planted in earlier years will bear fruit—that's what it's about—but it can take a long time.' So try not to agonize over every outbreak of temper or be too judgmental of her contrary moods. And always allow yourself to be convinced by a good counterargument!

Strict? Or laid back?

Talk to other parents, listen and learn from their experiences. Doubtless, you will think that some parents are too rigid and have too many rules, while others are too laid back and don't have nearly enough rules. Set age-appropriate boundaries, but be willing to be flexible. Exceptions can sometimes be appropriate. For example, if you've established that your daughter isn't allowed to go to an all-day music festival on her own until she's sixteen, if she has an older brother with her, or is accompanied by the parents of a girlfriend, then perhaps fifteen is fine. **If you forbid too much, there's a risk you will be lied to or that your daughter will rebel against every limit you set.**

My advice is to keep talking with her. Express your opinions, share your concerns and fears, but make sure you *listen* when she responds to you!

✦ ✦ ✦ ✦ ✦ ✦ ✦ ✦ ✦ ✦ ✦ ✦ ✦ ✦ ✦ ✦

Setting limits, showing trust
by Steve Biddulph

The aim of parenthood is that one day your child will be an adult who can handle the real world. She will know when to say no to another drink, she will know when to leave a situation where there is unwanted sexual attention or physical danger, she will know when she needs to sleep and when to eat nourishing food. She will know how to balance work and play, how to differentiate friendship from lust, and how to separate loyalty from being taken for granted. But these are complicated issues, which every adult (even ourselves!) sometimes has trouble with. So nature allows about ten years to learn them, and these years are called adolescence.

The job of the parent of an adolescent girl is to give her the tools and skills she needs to navigate this period of time and emerge into adulthood. This is a gradual process, fraught with trial and error, and requires constant communication and vigilant observation.

Parents get limit-setting wrong when they lean too far in favor of freedom or too far in favor of restriction. Here are two stories that illustrate this point.

David and Ellie held a party for their fifteen-year-old daughter, Jennifer, a student at an expensive private school. They decided to give the kids 'space' and didn't supervise the party, but retreated upstairs to another part of the house. So they didn't notice when one of Jennifer's girlfriends collapsed on the front lawn at 1 a.m. from alcohol poisoning. Thanks to the superior care she received in the intensive care unit at a local hospital throughout her sixteen-hour coma, she emerged from the ordeal unscathed. But for David and Ellie, it was a nightmare they'll never forget.

Patrick and Angelina took the opposite approach, and never allowed their seventeen-year-old daughter, Rebecca, to go to parties for fear of drinking and drugs. In addition, they were reluctant to let her go to friends' houses, and fretted constantly over her diet, clothes, homework and grades. When Rebecca's friends visited, Patrick and Angelina plied them with food, hovering anxiously, and tried to engage them in conversations that soon had them fleeing, never to return. When Rebecca turned eighteen, she ran away from home with an unemployed drummer and was pregnant within three months. Patrick and Angelina didn't see their daughter for two years.

These are the kinds of stories that make it clear that some kind of 'middle road' approach is the sanest and safest path to take. If you think you're already taking a middle road approach, you've probably also realized you'll need a strategy for encouraging and reinforcing self-sufficiency in your daughter, gradually and in a way that is suitable to her age and stage of life.

Some guidelines:

✦ Girls are not mature enough to handle sexual pressure (their own, or from boys) until at least age sixteen or seventeen, and sometimes not even then. So, unsupervised parties, or mixed outings without adults around, should be approached with a lot of care.

✦ Trust isn't the same as wishful thinking, it's based on experience. 'We trusted you to be home at 11 o'clock on Friday night, and you did that just fine. So you can go to your friend's house again next week.' Or 'You said you'd get a ride home from soccer practice with Jenny's mom, but her brother drove you home instead. That's not what we agreed. If you want to go to Jenny's house this weekend, you have to phone us, and we'll come and get you. It's a long way, so you can pay us back by making dinner one night next week.'

The idea is very clear, and as old as time itself: Freedom is something you earn. There's no need to be too rigid or inflexible about it, as it should be a friendly and light-hearted thing, but it is a real issue all the same. Adults are people who pull their weight. Teenagers are young people who are learning to pull their weight. The message to send your teenage daughter is: The more responsible she can be, the more responsibility she can have.

Remember, this is still a young person you are dealing with, prone to misjudging or overestimating herself. Do it in baby steps.

✦ When you need to get your point across, use 'I' statements rather than attacking your daughter with blame and shame. 'I was scared and couldn't sleep when you didn't call to say you'd be late. I didn't know if I should ring the police. You are so precious to me. I don't want to go through that again. I need for you to know that I want you to call me, even if it's the middle of the night and you think I'll be mad. Just call me if you get into trouble. No questions asked. I'll always come.'

✦ Arguing is the process of sorting out the issues of adolescence and a hallmark of the teenage years. Be good-natured about it, and don't take it personally. If your daughter seems to debate with you about everything, it means she's on track. The frontal cortex of the brain is growing during this stage when teenagers can seem unbelievably dense and obtuse at times. By discussing and arguing and debating, as long as it's not too heated, they are actually programming rational thought back into their brains.

✦ It helps if they know you love them. Watch the ratio between seriousness and fun, criticism and praise, warmth and firmness. The aim is for your daughter to feel that you like her, and that you love her. Take advantage of any opportunity to have fun together every day, no matter how slight the pretext: turning up the radio when a good song comes on, and dancing around the kitchen while you clean up after supper; enjoying a silly commercial on the television; interrupting her homework for a few minutes with a joke, a hug and a snack.

✦ Some families are so busy following their impossibly packed schedules—band practice, dental appointments, extra credit projects, math tutorials, weekend chores—it's enough to depress any teenager. Kids need some time off to decompress from the pressures of school and parental expectations. Teenagers in particular need time to do nothing, to daydream.

If you are very stressed by your own life, or your daughter's, you are likely to make matters worse, and seeking help from a professional counselor can sometimes help. They can offer emotional support and a sense of perspective. Also, don't forget to mine the expertise of friends who have already been through the teenage years with their children and compare notes.

But the very best thing you can do for yourself and for your daughter is to slow your life down, relinquish some responsibilities and commitments, so that when the unexpected comes along, you have some reserves of calm and strength and creativity for handling it. After toddlerhood, the early- to mid-teen years will be the most challenging period of your daughter's childhood. This is when she will need you the most. You *have* to be available and committed. Your daughter's adolescence is not the time for you to take a back seat.

But it can also be fun, and the reward is a fantastically capable young adult.

✦ ✦ ✦ ✦ ✦ ✦ ✦ ✦ ✦ ✦ ✦ ✦ ✦ ✦ ✦ ✦ ✦ ✦ ✦

Staying on track

With the onset of puberty, there is a percentage of straight-A girls who will let their grades slide. This is somewhat understandable when you consider the drastic physical and emotional changes they're going through. Patience and understanding are what these girls need; disappointment, punishment and pressure are not. (It is a sobering fact that many teenage girls commit suicide apparently because their academic achievements don't satisfy their parents. Although statistically more boys than girls kill themselves, all parents need to take this issue seriously.)

Children must learn to take responsibility and the best way to instill this concept is with positive reinforcement. Make it a rule that if your daughter doesn't finish her homework and chores, she can't claim certain privileges. 'You may go to the movies, but your homework must be done beforehand.' Or 'I'll drive you to your girlfriend's house if you clean your aquarium first.' However, bargaining for responsible behavior doesn't always work, and you may find you need support. Talk with your partner, with your daughter's teachers, with other parents, or with a therapist or school counselor. Sometimes an outsider can see what is going on more clearly than you can, and can contribute solutions from a fresh perspective.

For lots of teenage girls, school is primarily the place where they meet their girlfriends—and their boyfriends. It's also the place where they learn to take on challenging tasks and follow through on them. Take, as examples, the enormous commitment young people display when they're preparing for a theatrical performance or running a fundraising project.

When a crisis is an opportunity

Growing into the adult world is the most difficult phase in life. Therefore, it should not surprise anyone that many young people experience some sort of crisis during this period. Girls need a strong parental influence during this period, but 'strong' meaning a parent or parents who know what their beliefs are and stick to them, not 'strong' in the sense of bossy and intractable. Your daughter should know where you stand on moral and ethical issues, and she should know just how closely you will stand by those feelings—even if they are different from hers—but she should also feel secure in the knowledge that you will never leave her in the lurch, even when she makes mistakes. You and your daughter can only talk to each other really honestly when there is an unshakeable level of trust and understanding between you.

Try to remember that a crisis is always an opportunity. When your daughter dyes her hair blue, or gets a tattoo, or gets caught drinking or smoking, or gets her bellybutton pierced, or seems moody all the time, or is rude to your adult friends, or makes uncharacteristically poor grades, or shoplifts, or diets obsessively (and there are hundreds of other things I could add to this list), each event, major or minor, will shake up the whole family. It may be very difficult to see it, but each of these behaviors is an opportunity for change. It may be even more difficult to act on the opportunity, but it is a creative way to turn a negative into a positive experience for everyone concerned.

Family therapy, which is one approach to this sort of crisis, doesn't just help your daughter; it helps the whole family. Everyone is a winner when an individual's circumstance is recognized and acknowledged, when secrets are revealed and aired, or when complicated situations are clarified and handled. After a crisis has been successfully processed, family dynamics are generally more mature, more secure and more affectionate.

There are three particular crises that parents with teenage daughters are experiencing more and more: eating disorders, drugs and depression.

Eating disorders

It is mainly girls and women who suffer from eating disorders such as anorexia nervosa (in which a girl will literally starve herself of food) and bulimia (food is consumed, even binged on, but then deliberately purged by induced vomiting or laxative abuse).

Eating disorders are phenomena that occur primarily in Western industrialized countries where, ironically, there's enough money and food for everyone to eat their fill. Their causes vary from one individual to the next, and there are many excellent books and other resources that can help you sort through the complex and numerous reasons for these baffling syndromes. It is important to recognize the symptoms and *take them seriously.* These are *not* adolescent phases your daughter will outgrow. Rather, they are potentially dangerous illnesses that can be life-threatening.

Psychiatrist Dörte Stolle tells the story of Carina, a fifteen-year-old who suffered from anorexia nervosa. Carina believed that her little brother was her mother's favorite child, and thus Carina felt she didn't receive enough maternal attention. Her sense of isolation was compounded by the fact that she rarely saw her father, whom she adored. Thus on the one hand, Carina felt resentment that she was expected to be a kind of partner for her mother, and on the other she felt lonesome and not cared for. In an effort to gain some control over her situation, she stopped eating. When she dropped down to an alarming 88 pounds, her life was at risk and she was admitted to a pediatric psychiatric ward. With the help of doctors and therapists, Carina finally succeeded in getting her illness under control.

She wrote about herself, 'My parents were not role models for me. They didn't understand me at all, but always behaved as if everything was all right. In previous years, my father was always away on business; often we only saw each other at weekends. I think my mother wanted to replace him, and she tried to present a harmonious family picture to the outside world, but she was not happy, not even satisfied. I somehow had the feeling that I should have helped her. Sometimes, I thought I was not even her daughter, but her partner.'

Differences of opinion are normal during puberty, but does your daughter feel *totally* misunderstood? Does she feel that you can't function as a parent without her? If you suspect that she feels a disproportionate sense of responsibility, warning bells should sound in your head. Please consider family counseling *before* you face a crisis with your daughter.

Stay tuned in

If you listen to your daughter from the beginning, and if you allow her to express her feelings openly and honestly, chances are you can avoid a life-threatening mistake. Children, especially girls, are fundamentally cooperative by nature, and they sometimes hide their true feelings if they think their parents could be upset by them. Carina never said to her father, 'Dad, please stay here, I need you!' And she probably did not show her resentment toward her little brother either, because she wanted to be perceived as a 'good' girl.

An attentive parent might have seen from her behavior—before she stopped eating—that Carina was not doing well and could have taken some steps to find out what the problems were and maybe even solve them. If your daughter reveals her feelings easily and without inhibitions, be grateful! It's a superb survival technique!

Drugs and alcohol

Lisa also felt misunderstood by her parents and began to consume alcohol regularly by the age of thirteen. 'You'll end up on the streets!' her father shouted. He was the classic accuser who found fault with everything Lisa did and predicted dire consequences to follow. Her mother was the exact opposite and attempted to sweep every unpleasant or uncomfortable incident under the carpet, and was determined to look the other way when Lisa drank. The façade, that everything was just fine, had to be kept intact.

154 ◆ Raising Girls

Lisa felt torn between her parents. Her mother was a poor role model who avoided facing the truth. Her father could have been a better role model, because he at least was not afraid to face reality and express himself. But his punishments were severe and his opinions extremely harsh and belittling to his daughter.

After a number of sessions with a family counselor, both parents managed to improve their own behavior as individuals and as a couple. Lisa's father was able to give her more space, while still expecting her to follow certain rules—including not drinking alcohol. He also (finally) gave her the positive attention and time she craved, and became more supportive overall. The relationship between father and daughter improved dramatically. Lisa's mother began to express her feelings and opinions more often and showed Lisa that she did care enough to get involved, even if it meant admitting that everything wasn't perfect. However, she supported her husband when he insisted that Lisa stick to the new rules.

Sooner or later during puberty, many girls will experiment with drugs, alcohol and cigarettes. As parents, you will probably not be able to prevent this, but what you can do is lead the way by setting good examples and expressing your opinions. The message you need to convey to your teenage daughter is: 'We're here for you and we'll stand by you, even when you do something we don't like or approve of.'

Depression

There are many causes for adolescent depression, including the break-up of a friendship or romantic attachment, the death or serious illness of a family member, parental divorce, academic pressure or failure at school, and rejection by a peer group. Any of these can lead to mild or deep depression, sometimes even to suicide. Depression is also often associated with anxiety. Every parent should take the early warning signs of depression very seriously.

How do you know if your daughter is clinically depressed? Indications include:

- ✦ depressed or irritable mood

- ✦ diminished interest or pleasure in most activities

- ✦ significant change in weight or appetite

- ✦ insomnia or hypersomnia

- ✦ fatigue or loss of energy

- ✦ feelings of worthlessness or guilt

- ✦ impaired thinking, concentration or decision-making

- ✦ thoughts of not being here any more

If your daughter has five or more of these symptoms for two weeks continuously, there is a possibility that she is suffering from a depressive illness. Girls suffering from depression seldom reveal it explicitly to others. They tend to have few or no girl-friends, and often withdraw into themselves. Sometimes she will 'confide' in a pet, such as a dog, cat or horse, in a way that she won't to another person. Keep communicating with your daughter, even if you think she isn't listening. One-sided chats that offer solutions and convey hope and trust may be more helpful than you realize. However, if you are at all concerned, consider seeking some professional help.

Self-defense and its benefits

A self-defense course not only helps women and girls protect and defend themselves in violent situations, it can help instill a sense of confidence, competence, capability and strength in *any* situation. Self-defense classes coach girls on how to assert themselves, how to occupy a space, how to defend a position or a point of view. So, self-defense is not only about physical ability; it's also a mental stance that says, 'I'm allowed to stand my ground!'

Help your daughter to feel confidence and joy in physical movement and expression. Find out what's available in your area. Aikido, judo and karate are martial arts that take many years to master. These ancient traditions not only strengthen the whole body, they also teach respect for the opponent. When you bow to your fellow combatant before and after each bout, you are expressing respect and reverence for them. After all, it is only through and with an opponent that you can learn and progress within yourself.

There are also short-term self-defense courses that teach special fighting tactics and survival strategies. These are often offered though local law-enforcement or community services and don't require a long-term commitment to years of training.

The difference physical self-confidence can make

Nicky Marone tells a true story about twenty-one-year-old Ginny, who worked the evening shift at a restaurant. She was a small and petite woman who worried about walking to her car in the dark after work. One night, she noticed a man lurking close to her car. Although she was terribly frightened, she decided to muster all her courage and defend herself. First, she threw her handbag to the ground, then she took up a classic self-defense posture with her feet braced wide apart, her weight evenly balanced, fists held up. She yelled, 'Hey, you, I don't know what you want or why you're here, but I'm telling you, it's not going to be easy for you! I'm ready for you!' For a few endless moments, they faced each other. Then the man turned around and left.

Ginny attributed her survival instincts to her father. As the second daughter (not the hoped-for son that had been expected), Ginny accompanied her father on fishing and hunting trips, practiced arm wrestling with him, and showed an avid interest in car repair and other mechanical jobs that her father was proud to teach her. Thus, throughout her childhood, Ginny identified with male behavior patterns. Marone writes, 'Ginny would most likely have become a victim had she not learnt how to behave aggressively. Regrettably, aggressive behavior is not encouraged for women.'

In a nutshell

✦ Teach your daughter about the physical changes that accompany the onset of puberty. Also explain the surprising and confusing emotional changes that can also occur.

✦ Be open about discussing menstruation, and treat it as something to celebrate rather than something to be ashamed of or embarrassed about.

✦ Stay connected with your daughter as she moves into her teens.

✦ When it comes to setting limits, striking the right balance between freedom and restriction will help to give her a sense of personal responsibility while still keeping her safe through these tricky years.

✦ Research the warning signs for eating disorders, drugs and alcohol abuse, and depression. If you sense something is wrong, it probably is. Look for symptoms and take them seriously. Your daughter's life is depending on it.

✦ Acquiring some self-defense skills will help your daughter's self-confidence as well as improve her physical safety.

The power of the maternal instinct —Micky

May (four), Cristina (seven) and I (their mother) were out walking in the bush one beautiful winter's day. I had for some time been thinking, about safety, control, independence and letting go. I watched my gorgeous girls roam and play, laugh and banter, and I decided to let go of all those thoughts and just enjoy the day. We were on our way to Turtle Creek to see if we could spot any turtles.

'Let's run!' Cristina suggests when we get closer to a bridge crossing the creek. May doesn't need any more encouragement than that and heads off. Within minutes we reach the bridge, out of breath. It has recently rained, so everything is wet, green and sparkling. The creek is muddy after all the rain. I feel happy and blessed with all this beauty.

May steps up onto a log running along the edge of the bridge. I open my mouth to tell her to step down, but I am way too late. All I see is a little green arm vanish into the muddy waters several yards below us. Before I can give any rational thought to my actions, I scream, quickly scan the banks, which are heavily overgrown with lantana, and pull off my boots and my thick woolly sweater. I have no conscious thought of this, and am later surprised to find my sweater jumper on the bridge.

I look down. No sign of May. I crawl down the side of the bridge to find a spot I can jump from, well away from where May fell in so I don't land on her. I feel very strong. I swing out

(continued)

and let go. Thankfully, there is nothing but water under me when I land; no rocks, no logs, and no May.

No May! Where is she? I start to panic. The worst-case scenario runs through my brain like a wild and hellish nightmare. I can't go underwater to look for her because there is no visibility. I start to feel around in the water with my hands in the hope of finding an arm or a leg, anything to drag her up by. My heart is pounding and I have started to sob. I cannot lose my child. I cannot. I cannot. I cannot.

Suddenly, I feel something other than water running through my fingers. I grab hold of it and in a second my life changes again. Spluttering and coughing and crying, May is in my arms. I hug her and hug her, probably squeezing the remaining water out of her lungs. She is here, she is back, she is alive!

How we got out of the creek and back home is a mystery to me. I remember nothing of it. What I do remember is Cristina looking up at me with big, blue, laughing eyes and saying, 'Mum, you swung off that bridge like a monkey!'

Chapter 8

Relationships in the Family

Mother-daughter relationships are different from father-daughter relationships. Both are close, ideally, but they serve different purposes in a girl's development.

The relationship between a mother and her daughter is unique and intense. The Russian *matrioshkas* (the colorful rotund wooden dolls-within-dolls-within-dolls) clearly represent the close, generational relationship of one woman emerging from another. Most moms and daughters have a strong relationship from the very beginning, due in part to the simple biological fact that women personally experience nine months of pregnancy. Many fathers have told me that their baby became 'real' for them at the precise moment of birth; for other dads, a strong bond with their daughter was not instantaneous, but grew beautifully over time.

Mothers and daughters

Mother-daughter relationships are not always close. The relationship of a woman to her own mother plays a role in this. Sociologist Marianne Krüll gives us an example of how this relationship can affect the next generation: 'My mother treated her mother condescendingly and scornfully. I learnt, through her, that it is normal for a daughter to scorn her mother. My mother provided me with a model for this, so the way she handled her own mother was the way I behaved towards her twenty years later.'

Sometimes, a mother who feels she did not fulfill her education goals or career or job potential will push her daughter to do whatever it was she herself missed out on. With the best of intentions, an expectation is placed upon the daughter that does not match the girl's own needs. A girl who would prefer to play softball may be forced to learn piano or take ballet lessons. She might feel as if she is living her life wearing a straitjacket, and might take a big, painful swing at freedom when she's a little older.

A woman whose own mother gave little or no love will sometimes find it hard to be demonstratively loving herself. These mothers are sometimes labeled 'unnatural' mothers. However, this is unfair, because in such cases there is always an 'unnatural' child, too, that is, a child who was neglected. If the entanglement and pain remain hidden and unacknowledged below the surface, the unaffectionate behavior will be handed down from mother to daughter from generation to generation. But when a woman can clarify and safely explore her own feelings and fears and desires through therapy, a new healing path may be found and the cycle can be broken.

In so many discussions with mothers about their daughters, I have detected resentment, envy, anger, even hatred. (The story of Snow White illustrates this problem.) If you feel that you simply can't get through to your daughter, and you despair over her behavior, it might be useful to have a look at your own mother-daughter relationship. Get recommendations for a good family therapist, and choose the style of therapy you feel most comfortable with. Why wait? We are living in a time and a place where the possibility of healing exists.

Examining the baggage we bring into motherhood with us is the first step toward healing. Mourning and acknowledging our losses can help us see our children through different eyes. It might be both fun and constructive for you and your daughter to play or paint together. Your daughter would have the chance to express and work through some of her feelings in games or pictures. Fairy tales and stories can also be helpful. It doesn't really matter what you choose to do with her as long as the process helps you let go of the idea that your daughter must be the way you want her to be. If you suspect this idea is left over from your own childhood, it could be that this was the approach taken by your own mother.

If, however, you experience a deep, clear connection to and love for your daughter, you will probably navigate her childhood with few crises and solve your small, everyday conflicts with humor and sympathy and common sense—at least until she hits puberty.

A family history lesson

Tell your daughter about the women in her family—her mother, aunts, cousins, grandmothers, great-grandmothers—as far back as you can. Find out what they accomplished, great and small. 'I remember so much of what my grandmother told me in the kitchen,' says my friend Angela. 'She had a close bond with nature, grew her own vegetables, and knew a lot about nutrition.' I think it's important to keep this kind of female wisdom alive and to pass it on to our daughters. Historically, women

have been keepers of such knowledge and many other essential skills. Just think of all the beautiful handicrafts produced by women in the past—how they knitted, crocheted, embroidered, wove cloth and made lace. What do you know about these skills? Which of them do you have?

And what about our female forebears who worked outside the home, earning a living, which until recent times took courage and an intrepid spirit, and involved breaking down gender barriers and stereotypes? What have the women in your history handed down to you? It might even be worthwhile to visit a local library or museum with your daughter to find out more, and to refresh some memories.

The power of ancestors

Your past can give you power. Just imagine all the women in your family who have lived before you standing behind you on a winding staircase and giving you their blessing. What an empowering picture this is! Your daughter sees you as an empowering example to her every day. You're in a special position to observe the similarities and differences between you. By acknowledging those differences, respecting her and her preferences, paying attention to her fears and desires and valuing her for the unique individual that she is, you will help your daughter develop *all* her gifts and talents.

In some families, there is little or no discussion (or even memory) about those who have come before. If you come across forgotten members of your family, it can be very useful to investigate them. It can also be helpful to draw up a family tree, create an ancestral scrapbook or write a family memoir. These activities honor past generations and empower future generations by establishing a welcome place in your family's heart.

✦ ✦ ✦ ✦ ✦ ✦ ✦ ✦ ✦ ✦ ✦ ✦ ✦ ✦ ✦ ✦ ✦

Geza and Lena: A troubled relationship

Geza is a gentle person who dresses tastefully and always looks well groomed. But Geza has had problems with her daughter Lena, now seven, from the start. 'Lena was always crying as a baby,' she tells me. 'She wasn't happy with anything.'

Geza seems to think that even as an infant her daughter wanted to challenge her parents. Lena's father is self-employed and frequently works long days well into the evening. So during the day, Geza was almost always alone with Lena, and she became more and more angry with this screaming creature. Little Lena sensed her mother's frustration and disapproval, and felt rejected and unwelcome. Her response was to scream even longer and louder. 'It just never stopped, even when it made her vomit,' says Geza. 'As a two-year-old, Lena often just stood and yelled until she threw up.'

Now Lena refuses to do her homework and doesn't like to do any of her school assignments. 'She's unhappy about everything!' says her mother. 'When I go shopping for her, she always wants more of whatever I buy.'

In my opinion, Lena is fighting for her right to exist. She is deeply insecure; she doesn't yet feel that she is loved in a secure family. She has no idea that she can trust her mother.

It is pointless to criticize a child before you have established a trusting relationship with her. The simplest way to show a child your love and instill trust is by spending time with her, listening and talking and observing. In Lena's case, criticism about her behavior at school and at home just made her feel worse—and behave worse.

After a discussion with Lena's teacher, Geza managed to totally ignore Lena's school issues for a while, and instead worked on improving their relationship at home. For example, they started having afternoon tea together, and using the time to talk about their feelings. This little ritual opened some surprising doors and created a new sense of shared experience between them.

However, the relationship between mother and daughter remains problematic. Perhaps the pregnancy was difficult; perhaps the birth was long and traumatic for both mother and infant; or perhaps Geza had ambivalent feelings about having a baby to begin with. Although she is enthusiastically involved in Lena's school activities, and makes sure her daughter wants for nothing in a material sense, Geza is unable to create a firm bond or trusting relationship with her little girl. They don't trust their love for one another, and do not admit this, even to themselves.

If something is to change in all this, Geza must be willing to look at her relationship with her own mother and their relationship within the context of their family of origin. What does Geza bring with her historically that is having such a negative effect in the present day? What happened to Geza's mother and grandmother? Who was not looked after? Were there events that were kept quiet? Were there people who were not acknowledged? Or mourned? What steps towards healing these old wounds are possible today?

Weighing heavily on the story of Geza and Lena is the fact that Lena's father, who could have such a positive influence on his family, is seldom home when his daughter is awake. Thus she is being robbed of the chance to have positive experiences with men.

✦ ✦ ✦ ✦ ✦ ✦ ✦ ✦ ✦ ✦ ✦ ✦ ✦ ✦ ✦ ✦ ✦ ✦ ✦

✦ ✦ ✦ ✦ ✦ ✦ ✦ ✦ ✦ ✦ ✦ ✦ ✦ ✦ ✦ ✦ ✦ ✦ ✦ ✦

Tessa and Nina: Loving a daughter unconditionally

Tessa's title for her story about her daughter Nina is: The Great Surprise. 'She was so different from me, right from the start. At the moment of her birth, she emitted a powerful cry, and right then I knew that she would be a strong young woman one day.'

Tessa is a reserved, uncomplicated woman who places little value on material things and external appearances. So, she was especially surprised when her daughter, at the age of three, was already changing her clothes several times a day. And when little Nina discovered nail polish at a girlfriend's house, she went crazy for it. 'At four years old she wanted genuine leather shoes. She certainly didn't get that from me!' explains Tessa. 'And another thing,' she says, astounded. 'My daughter never hesitates to explain exactly what she wants, and then she insists on seeing it through— no matter what. It's exhausting, but I admire her for it.' Tessa is very different from her daughter in almost every way imaginable, but she accepts Nina the way she is and learns from her. And this attitude facilitates a solid and trusting relationship between them.

Like every mother, Tessa cherishes a wish for her daughter, an expectation: 'Nina will be strong someday.' Her desire has not had a negative effect on her daughter because there is no judgment or disapproval behind it. It is a positive statement through and through. Her attentive manner, and a certain curiosity about her daughter, allows Tessa to love Nina unconditionally. This is the most important prerequisite for a happy relationship between a mother and her daughter.

✦ ✦ ✦ ✦ ✦ ✦ ✦ ✦ ✦ ✦ ✦ ✦ ✦ ✦ ✦ ✦ ✦ ✦

Fathers and daughters

A father is the first man in the life of a little girl, and his role is vital. He represents the masculine, the fascinating 'other', and his daughter will compare every man who plays a part in her life to him.

If you (the father) and your daughter have a close relationship, she will probably choose men who are similar to you, although some women choose men who are in radical contrast to their fathers. For example, a woman who has had a difficult relationship with her father may look for a man who is very different in temperment and personality. And some women find themselves repeating patterns of experience and behavior from childhood in their adult relationships.

As with mother-daughter relationships, if the issues in a strained father-daughter relationship are not worked through and resolved, those issues will be passed from generation to generation. We know, for example, that a woman who was abused as a girl is vulnerable to enter a marriage in which she and/or her daughter will be abused.

The 'positive father complex' (see page 21) occurs when a girl admires, respects, loves and *trusts* her father. And, in turn, her father is consistently proud, supportive, understanding and encouraging of his daughter. It is important to remember that detachment of children from their parents occurs during puberty, and that it is an essential process for the transformation to healthy, independent adulthood. If detachment doesn't happen, a daughter risks spending her life in the shadow of her parents and will not develop her own identity. If her attachment to and identity with her father are particularly strong, her adult self-esteem may greatly depend on the extent to which she can win the admiration of men. You can easily picture the drama that occurs when such a girl loses her father, or such a woman loses her husband.

The woman who did not experience consistent parental love from both her parents in childhood, on the other hand, will suffer where her self-esteem is concerned. The kind of woman who feels unworthy of love will spend her life unconsciously offering herself as a victim because she believes that she doesn't 'deserve' any better.

✦ ✦ ✦ ✦ ✦ ✦ ✦ ✦ ✦ ✦ ✦ ✦ ✦ ✦ ✦ ✦ ✦ ✦ ✦

My father

My father certainly shaped the person I am. He was a kind man who always gave his children the feeling that we were wanted and that we were special with all kinds of abilities and talents. And he spent a lot of time with us collectively and individually. When I ask myself what made him such a loving father, I realize that at least in part it probably was because he lost his own father very early and, as much as possible, he wanted us to have lots of happy memories. Also, he was raised in a family with many sisters and female cousins, so maybe growing up among girls left him various 'female' traits and sensibilities, or at least gave him a better understanding of women and girls. And there was, perhaps, a third factor: he never had to go to war.

✦ ✦ ✦ ✦ ✦ ✦ ✦ ✦ ✦ ✦ ✦ ✦ ✦ ✦ ✦ ✦ ✦ ✦ ✦

These days, most fathers understand that they play a decisive role in their children's lives. Recently, I read with amusement that even fragrance manufacturers are reviewing and revising the 'new' masculine image. Men no longer need to 'prove' their manliness any more, their social focus has changed and they are more involved at home, with the family. (Maybe that's why they smell a little more feminine now too!)

✦ ✦ ✦ ✦ ✦ ✦ ✦ ✦ ✦ ✦ ✦ ✦ ✦ ✦ ✦ ✦ ✦

Which type of father are you?

There is the archetype of the authoritarian father who believes his wife must subordinate herself to him and that his children must be obedient. It doesn't take the gift of prophecy to see that his daughter will tend to see herself as a victim who will find it difficult to resist situations in which she is dominated by others, if she doesn't have a gutsy, rebellious mother as an alternate role model.

If you (as a father) recognize yourself here, ask yourself seriously what you've got to lose by encouraging your daughter to make a number decisions for herself rather than always deferring to you. Children inevitably and instinctively rebel against authority, so allowing your daughter some latitude sooner will save you much anguish and heartache later. Instead of resisting you, your daughter will learn to assert herself because of you.

If, on the other hand, you are a total softy who is adored by his daughter, chances are you also are being manipulated by her. 'If Mom says no, maybe I can still get a yes out of Dad.' You're not doing your daughter any favors by spoiling her as, later in life, she will no doubt experience bitter disappointment when she learns that not everyone will cave in to her flattery or tears or other various forms of coercion.

If you (as a father) fit this category, remember to demonstrate to your daughter that there are rules and limits, and that Mom and Dad will not let themselves be played off against each other. A father who isn't afraid to show his more vulnerable, emotional sides to his daughter will encourage her trust in return. She is far more likely to confide in him, share her decisions with him and consult him for advice later in life.

The true father
by Steve Biddulph

A 'true' father is much more than your child's friend. Your love, commitment to and involvement in your daughter's life is unshakeable. Whatever happens, you will be there for her, as long as you live. So, you have to be kinder, and more forgiving, than any friend would possibly be. Also, to do your job, you have to sometimes be tougher than any friend would risk being.

There will be times when your daughter will not like what you say, or what you do or what you insist she does. A true father expects and teaches his daughter to be a cooperative member of the family, who keeps her agreements, treats others with respect, is thoughtful in any situation and pulls her weight regardless of the circumstances.

Toughness, however, is not the same as meanness. Your daughter will be impressed by your quiet strength more than by your attempts to intimidate her. She will respond to your good-humored suggestions more readily than by caustic verbal criticisms. It is, ideally, a mutually respectful relationship, but not, for many years, an equal one.

What do children, especially teenagers, need from their parents? The security that comes from knowing that Mom and Dad stand on a firm foundation and can't be manipulated. By pushing against this firm family foundation, teenagers learn invaluable lessons about ethics and values, about compromise and standing fast.

One day, and sometimes at a surprisingly young age, your daughter will argue with you—and win! And, if you're honest with yourself, you'll find yourself thinking, 'I guess she's right!' At this point, you can choose to feel put out, or you can choose to feel proud that you have empowered her so effectively. (I once heard a father at a barbecue say to his teenage daughter, when a discussion became heated, 'I don't agree with you, but I think you're making a great argument!' Both father and daughter were aware of other people around them listening in, and she glowed with pride.)

So much of fatherhood is in the little things: like driving her to volleyball practice and watching from the sidelines, to comfort or cheer or both; knowing her friends and meeting their parents; helping her find a good photo of Kakadu National Park on the Internet at 10:30 at night while she frantically writes out her assignment due the next morning.

If you can work with her cooperatively and good-naturedly on a project (assembling a piece of furniture, for example) without getting tense and angry, then you are laying down the foundations for how she will do this kind of thing with her partner when she grows up. More importantly, you will be setting the standard for the kind of partner she will choose. If you are a remote or indecisive or uninvolved dad, she may choose partners who are distant or indecisive or non-participatory. These are pretty good reasons to work at being an actively good role model for your daughter.

Of course, you will have conflicts. But whatever time you spend in conflict with her needs to be done really well. If you are able to say 'no' to your daughter, kindly but firmly, with good reasons and no arbitrary rejections, she will not only learn how to hear 'no' reasonably, she will in turn learn how to say 'no' reasonably to others when she needs to. You can be much more effective in setting limits and getting cooperation if you avoid using hostility or fear tactics. A father doesn't bully, shout or intimidate.

Many women reading these pages will remember how their fathers launched humiliating tirades at them: 'While you are under my roof, young lady...' (as if we have a choice); 'You are a selfish, rude, inconsiderate, useless...' (maybe, but do you have to point it out at the cost of my vulnerable self-esteem?).

As men, we often seem to forget (or are careless about remembering) the fact that we are bigger, louder and stronger than our little girls and that physically *and* emotionally we hold all the cards. Our daughters long for our love, respect, admiration and praise. Which means every cut from a father goes very deep. The true dad is clear and firm, but he isn't aggressive. His underlying tone is warm, even when he is setting clear, firm boundaries. He takes his time, and listens to his daughter's side of the story.

Of course, this isn't always easy. It takes a lifetime of learning. But every inch of progress is worthwhile.

Imagine how it might be to really get this right. Our daughters, our little women in the making, will respect and love us, and will want to earn our respect and love and never, ever have reason to be afraid of us.

✦ ✦ ✦ ✦ ✦ ✦ ✦ ✦ ✦ ✦ ✦ ✦ ✦ ✦ ✦ ✦ ✦ ✦

The absent father

Cora has yearned for her father all her life. He is an American soldier stationed in Germany, and he has never seen her. In her imagination she has found her father, but in reality it has proved impossible. Children can be happy without their father, but something important will always be missing. Cora says, 'There is a permanent gap in your autobiography.'

Adopted children who, as adults, search for their biological parents express these kinds of feelings, too. Today, most people believe that children who are adopted have a right to know their biological families. Whatever the circumstances in individual cases, not knowing your 'real' mother and/or father can be very painful and may hinder the formation of a self-confident identity.

If a girl is raised without her father, it's important that she has other male role models in her life such as her grandfather, a close neighbor, a teacher or coach, or even an understanding stepfather. These relationships usually develop spontaneously and must always be entered into voluntarily.

A new man on the scene

If you, as a single mother, fall in love with another man and enter a new relationship, you might get lucky and find that your daughter warms to him fairly quickly. And he may be willing and able to take on a paternal role. But it's important that you never try to pretend that this man is your daughter's actual father. Ideally, he will become a good friend with some parenting responsibilities. If this scenario evolves while your daughter is still very young, then he may take on a more integral role than if your daughter is older, say, thirteen, especially if she lacks regular contact with her biological father. Of course, in such a situation there must be new rules regarding living together. And it's important to arrive at agreements that are realistic and that everyone can accept. With respect to your daughter's reaction to your new partner, just remember that friendship, respect and love cannot be forced. This applies to everyone in the house. What you should expect, however, is respect between your partner and your daughter. You and your new partner are the adults and therefore should set the example in this.

Recently, a desperate mother wrote to me complaining that her twelve-year-old daughter was stubborn, selfish and lacking any kind of empathy by turning a cold shoulder to the mother's new romantic partner. Well, what does she expect? That her daughter will be happy that her mother is newly in love with a man who is not her father? Honestly, this is not what I would expect from a twelve-year-old. And trying to rush or enforce a relationship between the daughter and the boyfriend is not a good idea.

For most children, a new parental partnership is going to be a problem, although they may not say so. You can help your child deal with this kind of new situation if you remember the following:

✦ Even after a separation or divorce, your daughter's parents are still her parents, regardless of whether or not the two of you get along.

✦ Every child has the right to love both her father and her mother. If your daughter is still very young, you will determine which parent she will live with primarily and what arrangements will be made to make sure she sees the non-custodial parent (if there is one) on a regular basis. The major criterion here should always be the best interests of the child.

✦ Disagreements between the parents seldom have anything to do with the children. Therefore, your kids must not be used as spies or as substitute part-ners. If you, as mother or father, feel that you were wronged in the relationship with your spouse, or that your children have not heard both sides of the story about the relationship, write down your side of it, and give it to your children to read when you think they are old enough to understand it.

When a girl loses her mother

When a mother leaves the family after a separation or divorce, or if she dies, her children are left with an incalculable loss. A surviving daughter loses not only her first great love, but also the person she identifies most with.

'What am I supposed to do?' despairing fathers have asked me. My answer: grieve. The loss of a partner is always painful, and if you don't allow yourself to feel the pain of that loss, you will make a tragic situation unbearable. The fact that some men find it hard to express or reveal powerful emotions like grief and fear can confuse children, and little girls especially. So, if you have suffered such a loss, talk to your young daughter about your feelings. Show her that you are not helpless and that you can deal with whatever emotions come up for you—and for her. If you have joined a support group of some kind and can talk about your loss in that context, you may find that it's not just you who benefits. Sharing difficult or overwhelming feelings with other adults who have had similar experiences may help you share those feelings with your daughter. Remember, you are not the first parent on the planet to handle such a loss. There is help out there for you and your children. There is information specifically geared to help you help your daughter deal with separation and death.

If your daughter's mother has passed away, don't be afraid to grieve *with* your daughter. Cry with her. Share memories with her. Allow your daughter to attend her mother's funeral, burial or memorial service. Give her the opportunity to participate in the event in a meaningful way, if she wishes it. Although there are well-meaning 'experts' who counsel against this, I think death is a natural part of the cycle of life and 'protecting' children from it only makes it more frightening. So be sure to allow your daughter to say her final farewells in whatever way is appropriate for her.

If you and your daughter's mother are separated or going through a divorce, hang a photo of your daughter's mother in a place of honor (yes—even if you are angry with your ex). Your daughter is her daughter too, and it will be important for your daughter to continue loving her mother, regardless of how the marriage or relationship ends. And, no matter what, do not badmouth your daughter's mother. If you choose to talk about her, focus on her good qualities, or on happy memories and mutually held opinions. Do not reiterate her less-than-stellar traits, or unfortunate experiences or areas of obvious disagreement. As parents, you will always be connected to this woman, no matter where your path as partners may lead you.

Brothers and sisters

There's an old saying that has a lot of truth in it: 'Brothers and sisters are like the salt in your soup—they are the spice of your life.' Siblings help shape us throughout our lives independently from the influence of our parents. While this is one of the eternal truths of family life, the way in which this shaping occurs may be undergoing a change as families continue to shrink in size. Whereas in previous generations it was quite common to have two, three or even four siblings, in much of the industrialized world today, the average number of children per family is 1.5, and the decision to have a second child is usually made well after the birth of the first. So, the majority of young children now have just one sibling with whom they experience the joys and sorrows of growing up. And in countries such as China where government population policies have been mandated, future generations of children will have no siblings, no aunts, no uncles, or no cousins.

✦ ✦ ✦ ✦ ✦ ✦ ✦ ✦ ✦ ✦ ✦ ✦ ✦ ✦ ✦ ✦ ✦ ✦ ✦

The only child

There is now considerable research debunking the traits that were once routinely ascribed to the only child. Today, we know it is unfair to assume that such children are necessarily spoiled, precocious or socially incompetent. Nowadays, due in large part to the economic necessity of professional day care, most children have plenty of opportunities to get to know other children and their families from a very early age. And with the rising rates of divorce and remarriage, 'blended' stepfamilies have become commonplace. Thus, a child needn't have biological brothers and sisters in order to be exposed to the social benefits of being around other kids.

✦ ✦ ✦ ✦ ✦ ✦ ✦ ✦ ✦ ✦ ✦ ✦ ✦ ✦ ✦ ✦ ✦ ✦ ✦

Birth order

Let's assume your first child is a girl. If a second child is born, the life of your first daughter will change irrevocably. If your second baby is another girl, chances are the two will naturally compete with each other, especially if the age gap between them is less than three years. Siblings of the same gender have to distinguish themselves from one another in the eyes of their parents, and most of them slip automatically into different family roles.

If the first child is deemed 'the smart sister', it may be hard for the second daughter to acquire the same label or push this quality to the forefront. So, she may instead become 'the sweet sister' or 'the popular one' or 'the wild child'. Such role allocations are extremely common and hard to abstain from completely.

However, if it becomes clear to you as parents that you have assigned a particular role to your first daughter, you can minimize the impact by making sure you don't reinforce it, and being careful in how you respond to the role(s) you see your second child taking on.

Your oldest child will be expected to be more grown-up. This is an inevitable assumption that she cannot escape from. The oldest girl also often slips into the role of babysitter, or even surrogate parent. Studies have shown that little boys and, especially, little girls will routinely turn to an older sister with requests for help, comfort and attention. In general terms, older sisters tend to be friendlier and more approachable than older brothers. An older sister will tend to 'naturally' care more about younger siblings than an older brother. Although many girls take on this role apparently effortlessly, in the long run, it can become exhausting, as it involves a level of responsibility that rightly belongs to the parents. Even oldest children are *children*, and every child has the right to be a child occasionally!

Birth order characteristics

The influence of birth order, or age position in the family, is generally considered an influence on personality and other characteristics, although the descriptions given below are by no means absolute or exclusive truths.

✦ The oldest child is more likely to be responsible, nurturing, a leader, a caretaker, critical, serious, bossy, independent, controlling, a high achiever, self-disciplined.

✦ A middle child may appear to be somewhat confused about their identity, may be a lower achiever, more of a follower, competitive, lacking in confidence, quiet, shy, a good negotiator.

✦ The youngest child tends to be more playful, less responsible, undisciplined, more dependent, often troubled by feelings of inadequacy, adventurous, friendly, creative.

✦ An only child tends to be self-sufficient, independent, a loner, a high achiever, selfish, intolerant, serious.

Research suggests that when seven years separate one child from the next child (older or younger), the environmental influences are considered to be similar to those for an only child.

We need to think of birth order characteristics in a general sense, and not take them too literally. However, similar personality characteristics that are consistent with respect to birth order have been found in adults and children and help us understand why we are the way we are. These characteristics are usually with us for life.

✦ ✦ ✦ ✦ ✦ ✦ ✦ ✦ ✦ ✦ ✦ ✦ ✦ ✦ ✦ ✦ ✦ ✦ ✦

✦ ✦ ✦ ✦ ✦ ✦ ✦ ✦ ✦ ✦ ✦ ✦ ✦ ✦ ✦ ✦ ✦ ✦ ✦ ✦

Mamma's boy and Daddy's girl

You cannot get rid of certain dynamics or sympathies completely, but beware that labeling and subdivision does not become too strong or too fixed. A key factor for living harmoniously together as a family? The generation gap should not be crossed, that is, parents are always parents, children are always children. When mother and son team up against father and daughter (or vice versa), for example, responsibilities become blurred and loyalties become confused. Parents must support *each other* in their crucial role as parents and present a united front to the children. A cross-generational alignment will make this very difficult and can all too easily lead to one parent undermining the other. Sometimes this arises from a sense of allegiance to a particular child, and sometimes the parent is being manipulated by that child. And it is not a huge leap to go from a sense of allegiance to out and out favoritism, which is another recipe for trouble. If you find such divisions emerging within your family, make a conscious effort to break this pattern. Spend some quality time alone with the child who is not 'on your side' and re-establish your relationship. Go out together, treat her to a favorite activity or sit longer at her bedside in the evening and talk with her. This child needs you, too.

✦ ✦ ✦ ✦ ✦ ✦ ✦ ✦ ✦ ✦ ✦ ✦ ✦ ✦ ✦ ✦ ✦ ✦ ✦ ✦

Different gender sequences

Parents with two daughters will be glad to discover that the two will tend to play together very happily quite often. A brother and a sister do not, as a rule, play nearly so contentedly with one another. If you allow each child to reveal his or her own individuality, and you accept each one as he and she is, the discord between brother and sister will tend to stay within reasonable levels.

All girls

If there are three or more girls in a family, and no boys, there's a possibility that one of your daughters will take on the role of a male child. She may even develop a number of 'masculine' qualities, because she is unconsciously making the effort to replace the nonexistent son. Children sense their parents' feelings very keenly and will often try to compensate for a parent's sadness or dissatisfaction or disappointment. If you are disappointed about not having a boy, discuss this with your daughters when they are at an appropriate age. For example, 'Yes, we would have liked a son, as well. But we've got smart, beautiful, healthy daughters and no family could be luckier! None of you has to play at being the boy. You are all perfect just as you are.'

Girl then boy

If your second child is a boy, your daughter will grow up observing the masculine from childhood, which may give her a fuller understanding of males later in life. The way you respond to your son will, of course, affect your daughter, for example, if you clearly favor him over her. However, if both children are secure in the knowledge that they are loved unconditionally, your family will survive the inevitable sibling conflicts.

Boy then girl

Conversely, if you have a son first and then a daughter, she will enjoy all the benefits, and trials, of having a big brother. And again, this dynamic can be quite rewarding if your older son doesn't have to struggle for parental love. Jealousy is an understandable and justifiable feeling. It's not a good idea to suppress it; in fact, it's best to speak about it openly. If, for example, your son feels jealous of the time and attention you give to his little sister and you allow him to express those feelings, he'll be less inclined to take out his frustration on her if you are compassionate and understanding with him. You could say, 'I know it's hard for you. We used to spend lots of time together, but now I have to also look after your little sister. I understand that you feel left out sometimes and that's perfectly normal. But you know, you are really special to me. You are so different from your sister and I love both of you in the same way you love both Mommy and Daddy.' If you are conscientious about making sure each of your children

feels valued, they will eventually learn to value each other and profit from their sibling relationships throughout their lives.

✦ ✦ ✦ ✦ ✦ ✦ ✦ ✦ ✦ ✦ ✦ ✦ ✦ ✦ ✦ ✦ ✦ ✦

Breaking the cycle of misery

The following true story clearly shows how conflict can be handed down from one generation to the next:

A mother has two sons. While she is pregnant with her third child, she visits an astrologer. The astrologer advises the woman against having her unborn child, because she says that after its arrival, the father will leave. The woman bears a healthy baby girl, but her husband dies the same year following complications after what should have been a simple surgical procedure.

The woman is beside herself with grief and sinks into poverty because the family has lost its breadwinner. She has to go to work, leaving her infant daughter at home in the care of her brothers.

The girl grows up adoring her brothers but suffers physical and emotional abuse from her overstressed, overworked and hate-filled mother. As she reaches young adulthood, it is wartime, and both her brothers die in battle. She searches for a husband who resembles her brothers. She finds him, marries him, and has a daughter, whom she abuses just as she was abused. The relationship between mother and daughter in this generation is poisoned, as before, by grief and bitterness.

But by the third generation, the daughter grows up in a time of peace and prosperity. She is able to understand and come to terms with her relationship with her mother. With the help of professional therapy, eventually, the painful cycle is broken.

It is important for parents to realize that the lives of our children are never really under our control, and none of us can accurately foretell the future of our families.

✦ When should we plan a second child?

✦ What impact does our handicapped son have on our daughter?

✦ We already have three daughters, and we'd love to have a son. How should we feel about this?

Instead of worrying about these sorts of issues, it is more sensible to look for the gift or the lesson contained in every problem. Things are the way they are. What we make of them is entirely up to us.

In a nutshell

✦ Mother-daughter relationships are sometimes troubled, but will improve if the mother comes to terms with whatever baggage she still carries from her youth.

✦ Tell your daughter about her family heritage, especially the women. Her forebears may be a source of pride and inspiration to her.

✦ A father is usually the first man in a girl's life, and so becomes the gold standard against which she will measure all future men. Don't undervalue this vital relationship.

✦ Siblings and birth order play a crucial role in a girl's development.

Parents sometimes need a little help —Mike

Not too long ago, my wife and I were concerned about all the arguing going on between our two daughters, Jenny (11) and Lisa (8). Jenny is a caring person but, like any older sibling, makes critical comments about Lisa's competency. Lisa is a very sensitive and emotional girl, and takes these criticisms completely to heart. Lisa is, in fact, very competent, but she has extremely high standards for herself and can become highly self-critical.

So, we went to see a family therapist, and were told that, despite our concerns, our problem rated pretty low on the scale of family dramas, which was good to hear. We now hold regular family meetings where we can all air our grievances and discuss how the arguing in particular and things in general are going. It's not like we had a crisis on our hands, but sometimes an informed outside perspective can be invaluable as a source of both help and peace of mind.

Epilogue

My daughter is now grown up. When I think back to the day of her birth and follow the path her life has taken, a reverent astonishment overcomes me. When I look at our life together, I rediscover the uniqueness she brought with her, which is still unfolding today.

Our relationship was very close in her early years. For the entire first year after her birth, I did not work outside the home. And I really enjoyed being 'just' a mother. This sabbatical with my infant daughter was made possible by a girlfriend of mine who supported me financially. I shall be forever grateful to her for this gift.

Following that first year at home, my daughter went to a family day-care center, where there was a small group of other children. She seemed to enjoy being there, and our relationship remained very close. I was still nursing her, especially at night.

Until she reached school age, my daughter did not sleep through the night, but needed someone with her as she was falling asleep. Fortunately, she had a close relationship with her grandmother, which allowed me to return to work. Some of my neighbors predicted that my 'spoiled' child would never grow up to be an independent adult. Still sucking on mother's breast at the age of three! But I couldn't—and wouldn't—have changed anything. I had to follow my feelings.

At the age of three, she went to preschool. She still has many beautiful memories from that time, along with a colorful silk cushion and a tattered photo album, her farewell present. She also made her first friends there.

I have argued with my daughter ever since she took her very first steps. I can still remember how she came at me with clenched fists once when the ice-cream shop we were going to was closed! Yet we both always knew, and we still know today, that we can never be really angry with each other. Despite the differences between us, our connection is simply too deep.

When my daughter was four, we moved to the country. Living with animals and close to nature delighted her. At first she refused to go to the local school. So she stayed home with me and played alone while I worked. Of course, eventually she attended school.

As a little girl, she was extremely untidy. Her room was complete chaos! But she was also creative and capable. At the age of six, she painted her bicycle all on her own! But being able to *do* things on her own I knew was not the same as wanting to *be* on her own. And until her tenth birthday, I often sat at her bedside at night and sang lullabies to her. I believe the sense of security this gave her contributed greatly to her growing self-confidence and independence. During the years that followed, I played mainly a supporting role as a mother, while my daughter became an accomplished equestrienne.

As she grew older and entered her teenage years, she became naturally tidier. And for some years now, she has had a very pretty, self-decorated, and nicely organized bedroom. She even tidies up her girlfriends' wardrobes and make-up bags and cleans our house for pocket money. (My sons do this too, by the way.)

At seventeen, my daughter announced that she wanted to start traveling and felt ready to do this on her own. At first I was horrified as none of her brothers had become so independent so early, and I certainly never predicted that she would. But that's the way it is. And I knew it was the right thing to let her go.

I am so very, very proud of the self-confident young woman my little girl has become, right before my eyes.

References

Angier, Nathalie, *Woman, An Intimate Geography of the Female Body*, Bertelsmann, Munich, 2000.

Biddulph, Steve, *The Secret of Happy Children*, HarperCollins, Sydney, 1998.

Biddulph, Steve, *Raising Boys*, Celestial Arts, Berkeley, CA, 1998.

Bond, Geoff, *Natural Eating: Naturally Fit and Healthy*, Beustverlag, Munich, 2001.

Brett, Doris, *Annie Stories: Helping Young Children Meet the Challenges of Growing Up*, Hale & Iremonger, Sydney, 1997.

German Family Association, *Handbook of Parent Education*, Leske and Budrich, Opladen, 1999.

Focks, Petra, *Strong Girls, Strong Boys. Manual for Gender-Conscious Educational Theory*, Herder, Freiburg, 2001.

Gilbert, Susan, *Typical Girls! Typical Boys! Practice Manual for Gender Fair Education*, Walter, Düsseldorf, 2001.

Grabrucker, Marianne, *Typical Girls: Character Molding in the First Three Years of Life. A Diary*, Fischer Taschenverlag, Frankfurt, 2000.

Griebel, Wilfried and Röhrbein, Ansgar, 'What does it mean to be/or become a father?' *Handbook of Parent Education*, p. 315.

Grimm, Hans-Ulrich and Sabersky, Annette, *Open Your Mouth, Close Your Eyes. The Nutritional Guide for Parents and Children*, Droemer, Munich, 2002.

Grossmann, K.E. and Grossmann, K., 'Being a child on a South Sea island—childlike bonding from a cultural view', in Gottschalk-Batschkus, Ch.E. and Schuler (Hg.), J., *Ethnomedical Perspectives on Early Childhood*, Verlag für Wissenschaft und Bildung, Berlin, 1996, p. 283.

Hillis, Anne et al., *Yummy, Yummy, Yummy. From Mother's Milk to Children's Menu: Healthy Nutrition Tips and Tasty Recipes*, Beustverlag, Munich, 1999.

Jelloun, Ben Tahar, *Racism Explained to My Daughter*, Rowohlt, Berlin, 1999.

Kabat-Zinn, Myla and Kabat-Zinn, Jon, *Growing with Children: The Practice of Paying Attention in the Family*, Arbor, Freiamt, 1997.

Kagan, Jerome, *The Nature of the Child*, Basic Books, New York, 1994.

Kahl, Reinhard, *In Praise of Mistakes*, Pädagogik-Verlag o.J., Hamburg, Video, series 1–4.

Kässmann, Margot, *Upbringing as a Challenge*, Herder, Freiburg, 2001.

Kast, Verena, *Fathers-Daughters, Mothers-Sons: Pathways to Your Own Identity from Father and Mother Complexes*, Kreuz, Stuttgart, 2002.

Krüll, Marianne, 'Mothers and daughters', *Psychology Today*, July 2002, p. 20.

Lindgren, Astrid, *Fairytales* (complete edition), Oxford University Press, 1978.

Lindgren, Astrid, *Madita* (complete edition), Oxford University Press, 1992.

Marone, Nicky, *How to Father a Successful Daughter*, McGraw-Hill, New York, 1987.

Marone, Nicky, *Strong Mothers—Self-Confident Daughters: The Significance of Fathers in Upbringing*, Fischer Taschenbuch Verlag, Frankfurt, 2002.

Minker, Margaret, *The Moon Ring: Parties and Gifts for the First Menstruation*, Munich, 1996.

Oakes-Ash, Rachel, *Good Girls Eat Up*, Beustverlag, Munich, 2001.

Papousek, Mechthild, 'How can we foster the development of our children?' *Handbook of Parent Education*, p. 485.

Pease, Allan and Pease, Barbara, *Why Men Don't Listen and Women Can't Read Maps*, Pease International, 2000.

Pease, Allan and Pease, Barbara, *Why Men Lie and Women Always Cry*, Pease International, 2002.

Preuschoff, Gisela, *When Girls Become Women: The Book for Daughters and Mothers*, Herder, Freiburg, 2001.

Preuschoff, Gisela, *Small and Big Fears in Children: How Parents Can Help*, Kösel, Munich, 1998.

Preuschoff, Gisela, *Teddy Bear and Kitty Cat: Why Children Need Animals*, PapapyRossa, Munich, 1995.

Richter, Sigrun and Brügelmann, Hans, *Girls Learn Differently*, Libelle, Constance, 1994.

Schneider, Sylvia, *Nothing But Strong Girls: A Book for Parents*, Rowohlt, Reinbek, 2002.

Sher, Barbara, *Wishcraft: From a Pipe Dream to a Fulfilled Life*, Universitas, Tübingen, 2001.

Stolle, Dörte, *Developmental Crises in Girls*, Iskopress, Salzhausen, 2002.

Tannen, Deborah, *You Just Don't Understand: Women and Men in Conversation*, Random House, Sydney, 1991.

Index